D1420517

American Indian.

"BEFORE THE COMING OF WHITE MEN, we always had plenty; our children never cried from hunger, neither were our people in want," said Chief Black Hawk of the Sauk and Fox Indians. His words sum up the Indians' attitude towards the European invaders who grabbed the tribes' lands, plundered their villages and drove them further and further west.

Michael Gibson describes the first disastrous contact of two hostile cultures when white men stepped ashore in the New World, almost five hundred years ago. He explains how the Indian tribes fought in vain to keep their lands in the eastern part of America. A study of the life and customs of the Plains Indians is followed by the story of the Indians' experiences in the American West – between 1860 and 1890 they were decimated during the brutal Indian wars.

The Great Sioux Wars, which raged in the 1870s, culminated in "Custer's Last Stand" at the Battle of Little Bighorn. At the same time, the tribes of the Nez Percé and Utes were fighting for their homeland and very existence in the Rocky Mountains. They were cut to pieces, while the great Apache chief Geronimo led his people on a bloody but fruitless struggle against the U.S. cavalry.

But the story of the American Indians does not end with their last crushing defeat at Wounded Knee in 1890. The author takes the story up to the present day, and explains how Wounded Knee, 1973, came about. Throughout the book, he presents the facts fairly and impartially by drawing on both Indian and contemporary white sources. This is neither an "Indian's history" nor a "white man's version." It is an attempt to show how this appalling episode in American history could have ever taken place. The personalities of the Indian chiefs and the bleak and rocky landscapes against which much of this story was acted out have been brought to life by a wealth of contemporary photographs and lithographs.

1

Frontispiece Sitting Bull, chief of the Sioux Indians, in full ceremonial dress

The American Indian

From colonial times to the present

SURREY COUNTY LIBRARY
WITHDRAWN

Michael Gibson

ACC. NO. 18722
CLASS NO. 970 ·004
DATE 5·95
CHECKED

WAYLAND PUBLISHERS · LONDON
G. P. PUTNAM'S SONS · NEW YORK

SC-803055

Copyright © 1974 by Wayland (Publishers) Ltd.
101 Grays Inn Road, London, WC1.
All rights reserved. This book, or parts thereof, must not be reproduced in any
form without permission.

SBN: (England) 85340 3805
SBN: (United States) 399 11292 8
Library of Congress Catalog Card Number: 73 875 77

Printed in England by Page Bros (Norwich) Ltd, Norwich.

Contents

The Illustrations

Samoset, a Masasoit Indian, meeting the Pilgrim Fathers

Introduction

THE EARLY HISTORY of the American Indians is clothed in mystery. Archaeologists believe that their ancestors started to cross over from Asia to America between 20,000 and 50,000 years ago along a land bridge where the Bering Straits are today. In the following centuries, they spread from Alaska in the north to Patagonia in the south. Differing much in appearance, their only common features were black hair, brown eyes and some shade of brown skin. *America before the white man*

Before the arrival of the white man, North America was inhabited by a mere 600,000 Indians. They were divided into innumerable tribes, speaking many different languages. Their technologies were very varied. For example, the Sac Indians slept in bark wigwams, the Kiowa in skin tepees and the Pueblo in stone houses. Some Indians were hunters, others farmers. Some regarded war as insanity, others as the best thing in life.

The arrival of the white man in the sixteenth century revolutionized the life of the Indians. Their stone and flint tools and weapons were replaced by metal ones. The introduction of the horse had spectacular results. Until this time, the tribes living along the borders of the prairies were farmers. Even the Plains Indians were only semi-nomadic. But with the appearance of horses, which escaped from Spanish ranches in Central America and quickly multiplied to form huge herds, they abandoned their gardens and spent their lives hunting the buffalo. As a result, they had more time for religious ceremonies, dancing and war. Their camps and tepees grew larger now that they had horses to drag them across the plains. The horses became such an *Coming of the white man*

Ætatis suæ 21. Aᵒ. 1616.

Matoaks als Rebecka daughter to the mighty Prince Powhatan Emperour of Attanoughkomouck als Virginia converted and baptized in the Christian faith, and Wife to the Worꜹ Mꜰ Tho: Rolff.

Pocahontas, daughter of Chief Powhatan, converted to Christianity and married to Thomas Rolfe

essential part of their lives that they refused to believe that there had ever been a time when there weren't any. As the Navajos used to say, "If there were no horses, there would be no Navajos."

The first Indians to feel the weight of the white man's hand were the Aztecs of Mexico, who were conquered by Hernando Cortés and his small band of Spaniards in the 1520s. When the news of their victory and the riches of gold taken from the Aztecs reached Europe, adventurers from all nations set out for

Overleaf The coming of Christianity – a
church built by Spaniards and Indians at
Acoma Pueblo in New Mexico in 1629

the New World. Most of the *Conquistadores* made their way through Central and South America; a few turned to the north. Ponce de Leon landed in Florida but was killed by an Indian's poisoned arrow. Hernando de Soto led an expedition as far as the Mississippi, while Coronado explored the regions now called Arizona, New Mexico, Texas and Kansas.

Almost everywhere they went, these white men received a friendly welcome from the Indians. It is interesting that to the Spanish the Apache seemed "A gentle people, not cruel, and faithful in friendship (1)." However, the same could not be said of the Europeans, who treated the Indians with contempt. According to contemporaries, de Soto "was very fond of the sport of killing Indians (2)."

"A gentle people"

Soon, the conquerors were followed by settlers. The Indians of North America watched the arrival of the British, Dutch and French with misgiving. In 1607, a group of Englishmen sailed into Chesapeake Bay and founded Jamestown, Virginia. Next year, their leader, Captain John Smith, was captured by the local Indians but his life was saved by the chief's daughter, Pocahontas. Later, she married an English merchant and sailed to England where she died.

The Virginian Indians had a well-developed culture when the English arrived. They were organized in confederacies of eight to thirty villages recognizing one overlord. These paramount chiefs or "kings", as the colonists called them, lived with considerable pomp. When Captain John Smith was dragged before Powhaton, Pocahontas' father, he found him sitting on a low throne, wearing a rich mantle of animals' skins and a rope of enormous pearls. In summer the ordinary Indian warriors wore tiny breechclouts but these were soon replaced by warm leggings and buckskin robes in winter. In warm weather, the women made do with skimpy buckskin skirts, but the winter cold forced them to don thick gowns made of furs and buckskin. The men knotted their long black hair on top of their heads while their womenfolk let their hair hang loose down their backs. They adorned themselves with coloured paints and necklaces and bracelets made of shells or occasionally copper.

The Virginian Indians

The Indian villages were well protected against attack by high

The Flyer, an Indian dancer as seen
by John White, an early British
artist

wooden stockades. Inside the palisade were groups of large loaf-shaped houses supported by strong wooden frameworks and covered with skins and bark. Outside the village lay extensive, well cared-for fields, planted with corn, beans, pumpkins and tobacco. The corn was made into either a kind of porridge or coarse bread. They varied their diet with the fruits of their hunting, especially venison and wild turkey. They produced well-made "dug-out" canoes and were expert fishermen. They were equally adept at spearing, netting or trapping their fish.

Venison and wild turkey

They had a highly-developed system of religious faith and observance. They believed in the power of a "Great Spirit" and were served by professional shamans or medicine men, who painted themselves black all over and wore hideous headdresses made out of stuffed animals' and snakes' skins. Elaborate religious ceremonies took place in open-air temples with much singing and dancing and waving of gourd rattles. The colonists,

Virginian Indians dancing at their annual Great Feast

most of whom were passionate Christians, needlessly antagonized the Indians by knocking down their idols and treating their sacred places with contempt.

Fighting and raiding were a normal part of the Virginian Indians' life. The early colonists noted the skill with which the brightly painted Indians slipped through the forests and hurled themselves upon their unsuspecting enemies with hellish screams and shouts. Their favourite weapons were mighty clubs, spears, bows and arrows and stone axes.

15

16

Horowans, wife of Chief Pomeoc, and her daughter

At first, the English praised the Indians for their "tractable, free and loving nature without guilt or treachery." Indeed, for a number of years after Pocahontas' marriage, there was peace between the whites and the Indians. Enthusiastic colonists suggested in 1617 that a college should be set up to educate the Indians. James I approved of this project and authorized his bishops to raise funds for it. By 1622, the colonists had enough money to start building the college. But at that moment, the local Indians attacked the colony and massacred three hundred and fifty of its inhabitants, including George Thorpe, the manager of the college lands. The survivors were deeply shocked by the horrible ways in which the Indians had mutilated their victims' bodies, and abandoned hope of ever educating them. This attack was not unprovoked. From the beginning, some of the colonists had waged a kind of private war against the "savages," destroying their villages, burning their crops and murdering their people. As a result the Virginian Indians became disillusioned with the colonists and watched their steady increase in numbers with fear and disgust.

"Free and loving nature"

The great massacre of 1622 permanently soured relations between the colonists and the local Indians. Frightful atrocities were committed by both sides until the Indians made another full-blooded attack on the colony in 1644. When they had repulsed this at great cost to themselves, the colonists did their best to exterminate the local tribes. In fact, during the course of the seventeenth century, the Indian population of Virginia fell from 18,000 to 2,000. By the end of the century, they had ceased to be a serious threat to the security of the white community. Therefore, when the College of William and Mary was founded in 1693, the whites were prepared to provide places for some Indian students. However, few of the miserable survivors of these once proud peoples were prepared to take the opportunity.

A dying people

The New England Indians, the Wampanoags, the Pequots and the Narragansetts, were still in the stone age when the Pilgrim Fathers arrived in 1620. They used stone axes to cut down the thick forests which covered the landscape and then burnt the fallen timber, unconsciously fertilizing the soil with the rich wood ash. In this way, they produced large fields

Pilgrim Fathers

17

The Pilgrim Fathers and the Indians making friends soon after their first meeting

where they grew corn, beans, pumpkins, squashes, and water-melons. At this time, New England was thickly populated because of the abundant sources of food. The Indians were skilful huntsmen and made clearings in the forest where the deer came to graze on the luscious green shoots that sprang up from the decaying tree stumps. While they were quietly feeding, they presented the Indian hunters with an easy target for their bows and arrows. Both the rivers and the sea teemed with fish. The Indians boasted that even the laziest women could spin themselves hemp lines and catch enough fish to feed their families. Eels were so numerous that the Indians pressed them out of the mudflats with their feet and caught them with their bare hands. Large quantities of salmon and bluefish were shot with arrows as they swam upstream to spawn. The countryside was rich in edible roots and bulbs and fruits. The Pilgrim Fathers were delighted with the wild strawberries, raspberries and cranberries they found the Indian women collecting.

In some ways the New England Indians' culture seemed very primitive. For example, the Puritans noted with disapproval that during the summer the Indians wore nothing but breech-clouts, and were relieved when the bitter cold of winter forced them to wear more seemly clothes in the form of buckskin leggings, moccasins and fur mantles. During the winter, the Indians shared big longhouses which were made of oak bark and reed mats and contained several families, but in summer the families split up and stayed in smaller bark *wigwams*.

Although many of the early visitors to New England were captivated by the beauty of the Indian women, they soon discovered that the Indian warriors, especially the Narragansetts, were very jealous of their wives' honour and reacted violently to any familiarity. Nevertheless, at first, relations were very good between the colonists and the Indians. In fact, the Indians taught the Pilgrim Fathers how to till the soil and grow maize, or Indian corn. In gratitude, the Puritans invited the Indians to their first Thanksgiving Feast, and for once Indians and

Thanksgiving Feast

Spearing fish and drying them in the canoe – in the background, fixed traps into which the fish were driven

The Reverend John Eliot preaching to the Algonquin Indians

white men sat down in peace together.

Unfortunately, this happy state of affairs was soon to come to an end. However, at first the Pilgrim Fathers made a real effort to convert the Indians to Christianity. The Reverend John Eliot, the "apostle of the Indians," translated the bible into the local Algonquin dialect and persuaded many of the Indians to give up their heathen ways and join the Church. His converts, called "the praying Indians," came to live near the white

20

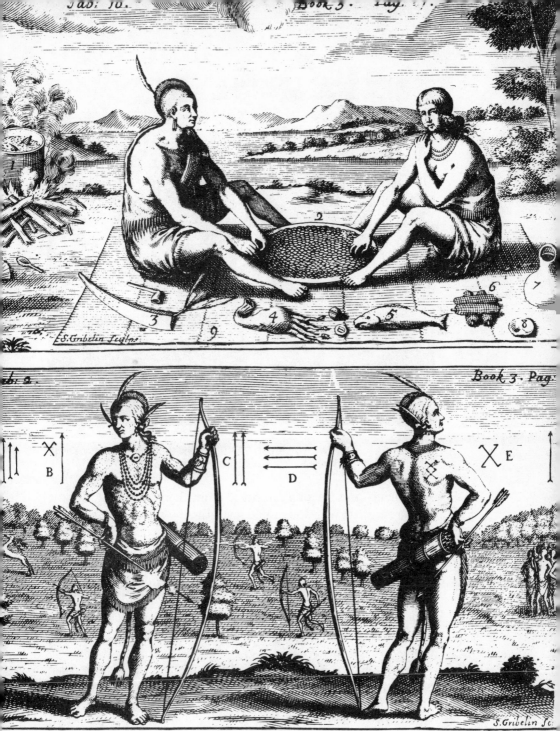

Top Two Virginian Indians at dinner. Notice the sweetcorn, which was unknown in Europe

Above A *Wer-o-ance* or chief of the Virginian Indians

A detail from a Pueblo Indian pot. The line from the mouth is supposed to guide the hunter's arrow to the buffalo's heart

settlements and became estranged from their heathen brothers. However, little was done to educate these converts. A few were *Indians at* sent to Harvard College when it was first opened, but without *Harvard* success.

As the years went by, the settlers pushed deeper and deeper into the interior and refused to pay for the land they occupied. Finally, in 1672, the Indians attacked the Puritan settlements under the leadership of Philip, chief of the Wampanoags. During the subsequent war, the Indians were defeated and their power broken forever.

Gradually, the British occupied the whole of the eastern coast of America with the exception of Florida, which belonged to Spain. British colonies were established in Maryland in 1634, North and South Carolina in 1663 and 1670; New Amsterdam was captured from the Dutch in 1664 and renamed New York; Pennsylvania was founded in 1681 and Georgia in 1733.

While the British settled the eastern seaboard, the French occupied Nova Scotia, Canada, and a strip of territory running from the Great Lakes to the mouth of the Mississippi. It soon became clear that the continent was not big enough to contain both these ambitious powers. While the Indians watched anxiously, the Europeans prepared for war.

Anglo-French Rivalry

1 Indians and White Men

THE EIGHTEENTH CENTURY saw a bitter struggle for supremacy between the British and the French. While they were locked in battle in Europe, their colonists in America fought with each other. Thus, while the War of the League of Augsburg (1689–97), the War of the Spanish Succession (1701–13) and the War of the Austrian Succession (1740–48) were being fought in Europe, King William's War, Queen Anne's War and King George's War were taking place in America. At the end of all this fighting, the British colonies had a population of one and a half million and the French some 90,000. In addition, some 400,000 Indians were scattered within the French and British territories.

The French realized that they could only hope to survive a full-scale colonial war with the help of the Indians. The value of Indian mercenaries was highlighted by General Braddock's defeat in 1755. Without waiting for Indian guides and mercenaries, he marched off with his redcoats to attack the French headquarters on the Ohio River, Fort Duquesne. On the way, he was ambushed and his force slaughtered by the French and their Indian allies. Thereafter, both sides tried to buy the support of the Indians.

Braddock's defeat

In fact, by the time the Seven Years' War (1756–63) broke out, most Indians had thrown in their lot with the French, who paid better than the British. As British reinforcements poured into America, they soon had reason to regret their choice. When the Cherokees attacked the British, they lost half their warriors. By the Treaty of Paris, which ended the war, the British became masters of North America. As a result, British colonists swarmed

Seven Years War

Opposite Sagoyewatha, a Seneca Indian chief who fought for the British in the American War of Independence, painted by George Cattlin

General Braddock ambushed by Indian allies of the French in 1755

over the Appalachians and down into the Ohio valley, where they settled. The natives were furious at this invasion of their hunting grounds and launched a superbly organized attack upon all the British forts in the area. They were led by Pontiac, chief of the Ottawa Indians.

Pontiac's rising

Lord Amherst, the commander-in-chief of the British forces, decided to exterminate the Indians. Officers from Fort Pitt (present day Pittsburgh) gave the peaceful Delawares some handkerchiefs from their smallpox hospital, wiping out the tribe in the ensuing epidemic.

It took two years of hard fighting to subdue the Indians, so the British decreed that there should be no more white settlement west of the Appalachians. However, on the outbreak of the American War of Independence (1775–83), the colonists defied the British decrees and started to move west once more. These frontiersmen had to face the fury of the Indians on their

Across the Appalachians

THE DISTRIBUTION
OF INDIAN TRIBES IN
NORTH AMERICA

ESQUIMAUX

KWAKIUTL
NOOTKA
NEZ
PERCÉ
CREE
MONTAGNAIS
OTAGUOTTONEMANS
ABNAKI
CHINOOK
BLACKFEET
ALGONQUIN
ASSINIBOINE
HURON
MASSACHUSETTS
WAMPANOAGS
WALLA-
WALLA
SNAKE
CROW
OJIBWA
IROQUOIS
MOHAWK
CHEYENNE
SIOUX
FOX
ODANDAGAS
UTAH
DELAWARE
SHOSHONE
PAIUTE
OMAHA
IOWA
ILLINOIS
SUSQUEHANNA
POWHATAN
ARAPEHO
SHOSHONE
UTE
PAWNEE
TUSCARORA
NAVAJO
MISSOURI
OSAGE
PAWNEE
CHEROKEE
HOPI
KIOWA
CREEKS
MOJAVE
YOKUT
APACHE
COMANCHE
WICHITA
PUEBLO
CADDO
SEMINOLE

AZTEC

own. They were tough, hardbitten men like Daniel Boone who discovered the blue grasslands of Kentucky in 1769.

When George Washington became first President of the newly-formed United States (1789), he realized that some kind of national policy towards the Indians was essential. Personally, he hoped that they could be assimilated. He even obtained money to equip them with domestic animals and agricultural implements, but it was not nearly enough. In any case, most of the Indians did not want to become farmers.

Lewis and Clark's Expedition
In 1803, the United States made "The Louisiana Purchase" from France and President Jefferson sent Meriwether Lewis and William Clark to explore the new territory lying between the Mississippi River and the Rockies. He told them to explain to the Indians they met that they came in peace and hoped to trade with them. They were well received almost everywhere. Soon, white traders appeared among the western tribes bearing trade goods, whiskey and disease. In 1837, for example, the Mandan Indians of the northwest were decimated by smallpox.

President Jefferson hoped to solve the Indian problem by persuading the eastern tribes to move beyond the Mississippi. But, led by Tecumseh, the great chief of the Shawnees, they refused. "Sell a country!" he exclaimed. "Why not sell the air, the clouds and the great sea, as well as the earth? Did not the Great Spirit make them for the use of all his children? (3)"

Removal Bill
The white man was not to be denied. On 28th May, 1830, President Andrew Jackson's Removal Bill was passed by Congress. As a result, most of the south-eastern tribes were forced to leave their homelands and move out west. And yet these south-eastern Indians had a long history of good relations with the white man. The "Five Civilized Tribes" – the Cherokees, Chickasaws, Choctaws, Creeks and Seminoles – had enjoyed a flourishing culture when the first white men set foot in America. They lived in solid houses made of wood, bark and reed thatch. They wove fine cloth out of thread spun from wild fibres and made beautiful clay pots. The warriors either knotted their hair on top of their heads or shaved it all off except for a scalp lock. Some tribes covered their bodies with elaborate tatoos but others only painted themselves.

28

A medal given by the British to loyal
chiefs during the War of Independence

Their tribes were divided up into clans and everybody traced their descent from their mothers not their fathers. Men were expected to go and live in their wives' villages after marriage. Their chiefs were elected by the whole tribe and could be removed by them if they lost their confidence.

As marriage was regarded as an economic bond, there were many "trial marriages" so that young couples could decide *Trial marriages* whether they were really suited to each other. Once married, however, the highest standards of morality were expected. For example, if a wife committed adultery, her husband had the right to cut off the tip of her nose and ears and to put her lover to death. Curiously, husbands were forbidden to speak to their mothers-in-law. This prevented a lot of quarrelling.

In spring, both the men and women worked in the fields planting the crops, but thereafter the women were expected to do all the hoeing on their own. At harvest time, the "Green Corn Ceremony" took place which was the most important festival of the year, signifying that the old year had passed away and a new one begun.

In spite of all their apparent sophistication the Five Civilized Tribes were as addicted to raiding and fighting as the rest of the American Indians. Their commonest ploy was to set their enemies' settlements ablaze with fire arrows and to pick off the frightened Indians as they tried to escape from the burning buildings. They showed their enemies' women and children no mercy and valued their scalps as highly as those of the warriors. As they saw it, the wives and children were hidden away in the middle of their enemies' village and therefore were the most difficult to get at.

Torture Amongst these Indians, torture was a refined art, practised mostly by the women. Their captives were tied to poles in the middle of the camps and tortured slowly to death. The victims remained defiant to the end. They sang their war songs and taunted their captors in every way they knew how to show that though their bodies could be broken, their spirit was as strong as ever.

Curiously, these fierce Indians came closer to adapting themselves to the white man's way of life than any others. Their chiefs were invited to the white man's settlements and met their governors and councils. A few even crossed over the Atlantic and met the king of England. The English saw them as powerful allies against the Spanish in Florida and the hostile Indians to

Torturing a captive by burning slow fires on his chest

Indians of the Five Civilized Tribes hoeing and planting corn

the west. Many white men married Indian women and settled down amongst them.

On the whole, relations between the Five Tribes and the English were very good until the American Revolution. The Indians copied the white man's houses, clothes and farming methods. They bought cattle and became successful stock breeders. They acquired ploughs and tilled the soil more intensively than ever before. They even started to grow cotton and weave it into cloth.

Then, after the defeat of the English, the Five Tribes had to try and win the support of the new Americans. They quickly realized that their only hope was to get themselves accepted as civilized people. As a result, they invited Christian missionaries to settle amongst them and open schools. Unfortunately, these mission schools did not prosper at first, because the missionaries could not discover a way of writing the Indian languages and tried to force the children to learn English instead. Then, in 1821, a Cherokee called Sequoyah invented a new alphabet, based on the English one. Within a few years, almost all the Cherokees could read and write. They even published their own newspaper. The other tribes soon followed suit. Soon, they were able to publish collections of their laws and draw up their own constitutions or systems of government.

The Cherokee alphabet

However, all this hard work was of no avail, because the

A full-blooded Indian general (second from right) on General Grant's staff in the Civil War

white man was determined that they should move out west. Many died from the hardships of their enforced migration, and others from the difficulties they met on the wild frontier. An army private wrote an account of his experiences at this time: "I saw the helpless Cherokees arrested and dragged from their homes, and driven by bayonet into the stockades. And in the chill of a drizzling rain on an October morning I saw them loaded like cattle or sheep into wagons and started toward the West (4)."

By 1838, eight years after the Removal Bill, all the civilized Indians had been resettled west of the Mississippi, in parts of what are now Nebraska, Kansas and Oklahoma. In spite of the hardships of the trek from Florida and Georgia, they were able *Indian* to rebuild their civilization in "Indian Territory." Agriculture *Territory* and commerce progressed, schools, churches and railways were built, and some white men began to consider admitting the area as a state of the Union. The Indian farmers even owned negro slaves, and it was this that helped their downfall. They supported the breakaway states of the South in the Civil War; after the Union victory, therefore, much of their land was taken away and given to freed slaves or white settlers. More and more Indians from Kansas and Missouri were settled on the decreasing area of land, and the old way of life slowly became impossible. Finally, when the state of Oklahoma was established in 1907, the Five Tribes lost their special position and faced the choice of losing their identity as Indians or living in poverty on the reservations.

Meanwhile, as the pioneers and settlers pushed still further westward, they entered the lands of the Plains Indians, proud, fierce people. These tribes were at the height of their powers and were prepared to fight for their lands. The great Indians wars were about to start.

B

—

2 The Plains Indians

AS THE WHITE SETTLERS made their way across the great Plains of America, they came into contact, often violently, with the Plains Indians. Of the many tribes who lived on the prairies, the Sioux, occupying the lands which are now the Dakotas and parts of Minnesota and Nebraska, were perhaps the proudest and the most numerous.

The Plains Indians

The Sioux were famous for their striking appearance. A young American historian, Francis Parkman, wrote a vivid description of a warrior he met in 1846: "He was nearly six feet high; lithely and gracefully, yet strongly proportioned, and with a skin singularly clear and delicate. He wore no paint; his head was bare, and his long hair was gathered in a clump behind . . . his chest and arms were naked; the buffalo robe, worn over them when at rest, had fallen about his waist, and was confined there by a belt. This, with the gay moccasins on his feet, completed his attire (5)." On special occasions, the Sioux chiefs wore splendid headdresses made of eagle feathers which hung down their backs.

The Sioux

Sioux women were tall and attractive. Parkman wrote of one woman who "had a light, clear complexion, enlivened by a spot of vermilion on each cheek . . . Her dress was a tunic of deerskin, made beautifully white by means of a species of clay found on the prairie, ornamented with beads, arranged in figures more gay that tasteful, and with long fringes at all the seams (6)." These dresses reached down to the women's ankles. They too wore gaily decorated moccasins.

Women

Indian children dressed like their parents. Parkman noticed

35

Opposite Young-Man-Afraid-Of-His-Horses, a Sioux warrior who later negotiated with the U.S. Government

that the Sioux "were very fond of their children whom they indulged to excess, and never punished, except in extreme cases, when they threw a bowl of cold water over them (7)." Sioux villages echoed with the happy laughter of the children, who went "whooping about the camp, shooting birds with little bows and arrows, or making miniature lodges with sticks (8)."

Children

The young boys stayed with their mothers until they were eight. Then they left home and lived in a group with the other boys of their own age. They were educated by the old men. Chief Luther Standing Bear wrote that his teacher never said, " 'You have to do this' or 'You must do that,' but when doing things himself, he would often say something like, 'Son, some day when you are a man you will do this.' (9)" The boys were taught to handle bows and arrows. The Sioux used short wooden bows, bound with sinew. Their arrows were flighted with three feathers. "Two red wavering lines, the symbol of lightning, were painted from the feathered end half way to the tip so as to allow the blood to flow freely from the body (10)."

Horsemanship

Good horsemanship was greatly prized. The little boys tried "to mount while their horses were running at full speed, running a few steps by the side of the horse, then grasping its mane, and springing in the air (11)." The girls rode as well as the boys.

As the girls grew older, they had to help their mothers with the housework. "Women's work," wrote Chief Standing Bear, "was to cook for the family, keep the tepee in order, and sew the clothing of the household members (12)."

Courting

When young people fell in love, the warriors mooned around the tepees of their loved ones and serenaded them with their flutes. Sometimes, young couples eloped, but more often than not they married according to the local customs. The husband-to-be paid his father-in-law a large brideprice, usually a number of ponies, to compensate him for the loss of his daughter. Among the Sioux, there was no marriage ceremony as such. The girl merely took her belongings and moved into her in-laws' tepee. However, in most cases, weddings were marked by feasting and the exchange of presents.

Among the Plains Indians, women were considered inferior to men, but they were not thought unimportant, in the way that

36

some white observers have suggested. Husbands usually felt genuine affection for their wives and took a pride in their appearance. Among the Sioux, it was usual for a warrior to brush his wife's long black hair each morning and to paint her face with red and yellow dyes. Warriors could have as many wives as they could afford. On the whole, the wives lived harmoniously together and shared the family chores between them.

Divorce, according to Chief Standing Bear, was "the simplest thing to be had and the most seldom sought for (13)." If a couple were unhappy, the husband could ask his wife to leave their tepee or she could go of her own accord. Standing Bear pointed out that "the one unforgivable sin in a Sioux husband was cowardice, and no woman would bear the humiliation of possessing a cowardly mate (14)."

The Sioux lived in leather tents or tepees. A framework of long wooden poles was arranged in a circle and covered with twenty-five buffalo skins, all sewn together. In summer, the covers were rolled up to let the wind into the tepee; in winter, they were weighted down with stones to make the tepee weatherproof. The women decorated the interior and exterior with paintings of birds and animals or geometrical designs. They made rugs for the floor and soft buckskin cushions, filled with cottonwood floss. Along the walls lay their bedrolls and leather bags called *parflèches* which contained all their personal belongings.

The Sioux could break camp quickly. Parkman recalled, "One by one the lodges were sinking down in rapid succession, and where the great circle of the village had been only a few moments before, nothing now remained but a ring of horses and Indians, crowded in confusion together. The ruins of the lodges were spread over the ground, together with kettles, stone mallets, great ladles of horn, buffalo robes, and cases of painted hide, filled with dried meat (15)."

The Indians piled all their possessions onto *travois*. These were pairs of lodge poles tied to the backs of horses and joined together by webs of ropes. On the move, the Indians presented an untidy spectacle: a mass of horses, mules and dogs, heavily laden travois, mounted warriors, groups of gossiping women and a

A Sioux horse-race

host of screaming children. Towards evening, they chose a new camping place. "As if by magic," wrote Parkman, "a hundred and fifty tall lodges sprang up. The lonely plain was transformed into the site of a swarming encampment (16)."

Much of the Plains Indians' time was spent buffalo hunting. When the white men first set foot on the plains, where were more than twelve million of these great beasts. "The face of the country was dotted far and wide with countless hundreds of buffalo," recalled Parkman. "They trooped along in files and columns, bulls, cows and calves . . . They scrambled away over the hills to right and left and far off, the pale blue swells in the extreme distance were dotted with innumerable specks (17)."

Even the young boys took part in this dangerous sport. "A shaggy buffalo bull bounded out from a neighbouring wallow," wrote Parkman, "and close behind him came a slender Indian boy, riding without stirrups or saddle and lashing his eager little horse to full speed. Yard after yard he drew close to his gigantic victim, though the bull, with his short tail erect and his tongue lolling a foot from his foaming jaws, was straining his unwieldy strength to the utmost. A moment more, and the boy was close alongside. It was our friend the Hail Storm. He dropped the rein on the horse's neck, and jerked an arrow like lightning from the quiver at his shoulder . . . The bull sprang again and again at his assailant, but the horse kept dodging with wonderful celerity. At length the bull followed up his attack with a furious rush, and the Hail Storm was put to flight, the shaggy

The Buffalo Hunt

39

monster following close behind . . . His eyeballs glared through his tangled mane, and the blood flew from his mouth and nostrils. Thus, battling with each other, the two enemies disappeared over the hill (18)."

At last, the bull collapsed and in an instant "The Indians were gathered around him, and several knives were already at work. These little instruments were plied with such wonderful address that the twisted sinews were cut apart, the ponderous bones fell asunder as if by magic, and in a moment the vast carcass was reduced to a heap of bloody ruins (19)."

The women filled horn cups with the warm blood of the dead animals and gave them to their children to drink. Whole stomachs were cut out and red hot stones placed in them until their contents had boiled and could be eaten. Parkman watched all this with some disfavour. "Some were cracking the huge thigh bones and devouring the marrow within," he noticed, "others were cutting away pieces of liver and other approved morsels, and swallowing them on the spot (20)." *Eating the Buffalo*

Much of the meat was cut up into strips and dried in the sun. Then, it was mixed with berries and bear fat and pounded into a substance rather like corned beef and stuffed into skin containers. This was called *pemmican*. In those golden days, the Plains Indians were never short of food.

The buffalo provided the Plains Indians with all the necessities of life, including "habitations, food, beds and fuel; strings for their bows, glue, thread, cordage, vessels to hold water, boats to cross streams and the means of purchasing all that they want from the traders (21)." Parkman added prophetically, "When the buffalo are extinct, they [the Indians] too must dwindle away (22)."

For most of the Plains Indians war was a way of life. Every *War* young man dreamed of winning fame in battle. No youth could be regarded as a man until he had performed a coup or deed of valour. Young warriors went into battle unarmed so that they could win the respect of their comrades by touching their enemy. As an example, when the First World War (1914–18) came to an end, the Sioux warriors who had served in the American army claimed entrance to their tribe's soldier societies

41

Opposite top Arapaho girls at Cut Hair's
camp on the plains
Opposite Where Great Herds Come To Drink,
painted by Charles Russell

on the strength of their military service, but they were rejected. Although they had killed enemies, they had not touched them so they did not count.

Success in war was rewarded in many ways. No Indian woman would marry a man until he had distinguished himself in battle. The most successful warriors became chiefs. The warriors recorded their deeds in the feathers they wore in their hair.

Killed an enemy

Killed & scalped enemy

1st Coup

Killed & scalped an enemy; received many wounds

Wounded by enemy; Killed an enemy

Cut enemy's throat

Received many wounds

Scalping

One of the most horrible customs associated with the game of war was scalping. All the Plains Indians and many white men collected scalps. Among the Indians, the centre of the head was thought to be sacred and to contain a man's spirit. A Sioux seized hold of a dead warrior's hair with his left hand and cut off the scalp with a sharp knife held in his right hand. Occasionally, stunned or badly wounded warriors were scalped by mistake. Most of these unfortunates recovered with little more than a livid patch on the top of their heads to remind them of their gruesome experience. Scalps were dried and displayed on top of tepee poles. Sometimes, a warrior had them sewn into the seams of his shirt and leggings. On returning from the warpath, they held scalp dances. The warriors circled their grisly prizes, leaping, stamping, yelling, rolling the eyes and contorting their faces.

Almost as popular among the Indians was horse stealing. According to Colonel Richard Dodge, who served in the

Scalping a dead U.S. cavalryman

American cavalry for many years, the Comanche were the best horse thieves. "I have known a Comanche," he wrote, "crawl into a bivouac where a dozen men were sleeping, each with his horse tied to his wrist by a lariat, cut the rope within six feet of a sleeper's person, and get off with the horse without waking a soul (23)." Most white observers were impressed by the Indians' love for their horses. Another cavalry officer noticed, "Every warrior has his warhorse, which is the fleetest that can be obtained, and he prizes him more highly than anything else in his possession, and it is seldom that he can be induced to part with

Horse Stealing

him at any price. He never mounts him except when going into battle, the buffalo chase, or upon state occasions (24)."

The Indians were famous for their horsemanship. A famous traveller and artist, George Catlin, witnessed a typical piece of trick riding in 1836. The Comanche warriors lay along the sides of their horses as they rode into battle. "In this wonderful position," he wrote, "he will hang whilst his horse is at fullest speed, carrying with him his bow and shield, and also his long lance of fourteen feet in length, all or either of which he will wield upon his enemy as he passes; rising and throwing his arrows over the horse's back, or with ease and equal success under the horse's neck (25)." [See jacket picture].

Many white men have claimed the Plains Indians were the most ferocious and dangerous people who have ever lived. Colonel Dodge wrote, "Cruelty is both an amusement and a study. So much pleasure is derived from it, that an Indian is constantly thinking out new devices of torture, and how to prolong to the utmost those already known. His anatomical knowledge of the most sensitive portions of the human frame is wonderfully accurate; and the amount of beating, cutting, slashing, and burning he will make a human body undergo without seriously affecting the vital powers is astonishing (26)." It is certainly true that the Plains Indians horribly tortured and mutilated the bodies of their prisoners, both red and white. However, it is only fair to point out that the white man also committed the most barbaric atrocities upon them. All that can be said in mitigation is that their hatred for each other was so great that any idea of mercy was banished from their thoughts. Torture was seen as essential for survival.

"Cruelty is an amusement"

Until the coming of the white man, the Sioux had no word for law. Their behaviour was controlled by custom. Chief Standing Bear maintained that "All matters that concerned the welfare of the band were taken care of in frequent council meetings where the chiefs and their aides met for discussions (27)." However, the chiefs did not give orders, they merely offered advice. When Chief Crazy Horse was asked what his tribe would do, he answered, "Ask my people what they want to do (28)." In fact, public opinion was the main obstacle to wrong-doing.

Law and Order

A shaman's rattle, used to give rhythm in the dance

Occasionally, chiefs carrying sacred peace pipes would intervene if fighting started among their own people, but even then they would not use force. The Sioux had no police. Their nearest equivalent was the Fox Society which organized big hunts and the movement of the village from place to place. Other tribes had "Dog Soldiers" who were responsible for the organization of religious festivals as well as police duties. After a murder had been committed, they tried to persuade the killer and his family to offer adequate compensation to the victim's relatives to stop a feud developing.

The relations between individuals were strictly defined. There *Kinship Laws* were some people with whom an Indian could laugh and joke and there were others whom he had to treat with the greatest respect at all times. Because of these kinship laws, everyone knew how he should behave towards everyone else.

The Plains Indians were also famous for their secret societies. Many were purely social in purpose. Their members learned *Secret* special songs, dances and games. Others were religious in origin. *Societies* For example, among the Sioux, the women's lodge or "Katela"

45

Top Blackfoot Indians perform the ceremony of the burning buffalo grass at the first full moon in June

Left A Blackfoot burial scaffold   Right A young warrior alone on the hill-top

re-enacted the deeds of the greatest warriors. The women wore red and blue dresses, carried weapons and even painted wounds on their bodies. They performed their dances in public amid great feasting.

The Indians were a very religious people. They believed that the world was full of spirits and was controlled by the Great Spirit or the *Wakan Tanka* as the Sioux called him. When a Sioux reached manhood, he set about approaching the spirits. With the help of a holy man, he built himself a sweat lodge so that he could cleanse himself. Once he was clean, he rode out to an isolated hill top. There he remained alone, naked except for his buffalo robe and without food for four days and nights. Carrying his sacred *calumet* before him, he walked up and down hour after hour praying, "O Great Spirit have mercy on me that my people may live (29)." As he got weaker, it seemed to him that the animals, the birds and even the wind spoke to him. At the end of his ordeal, his friends helped him back to the sweat lodge where he told the holy man about everything he had seen and heard, while the holy man explained what every incident meant.

The Wakan Tanka

There were a number of men in every tribe who experienced visions without any preparations. They were the medicine men or *shamans*. They had the gift of healing and could summon the buffalo and the rain. The rain makers, or Thunder Dreamers as they were called, "painted zig-zag stripes on their bodies to simulate lightning, as well as arrows and war horses, and were, unlike the medicine men, excellent warriors, many times using their powers to bring on a storm that would place their enemies at a disadvantage (30)."

Medicine Men

Indian life was punctuated by religious festivals in which dancing played the most important part. Among the Sioux, the most important ceremony was the annual Sun Dance, for as one warrior put it, "All living creatures and all plants derive their life from the sun (31)." The warriors cut down a fine cottonwood tree and dragged it into the camp with much singing, dancing and elaborate ceremonial. Then, the dancers purified themselves in the sweat lodges before erecting the sacred tree in the centre of the camp. When everything was ready, splinters of wood were

The Sun Dance

driven through the flesh of the dancers' chests and attached to the tree by long leather thongs. As dawn broke, the chosen few started to dance around the tree, gazing straight into the blazing sun and pulling against the cruel pegs in their chests. Eventually, after a period of terrible agony, the dancers tore the splinters embedded in lumps of flesh from their chests and were led back to the sweat lodges to recover. The Indians believed that by their suffering they ensured that the light of the Wakan Tanka would shine on them for another year.

"Somewhere in the sky"

The Indians believed in a life after death. A Sioux warrior called Chased-by-Bears claimed, "After a man dies his spirit is somewhere on the earth or in the sky; we do not know exactly where, but we are sure that his spirit still lives (32)." The memory of their ancestors was sacred to them and their resting places were hallowed ground. Chief Standing Bear described what happened when a man died. "The first preparation for burial was to paint the face of the departed as if for a festive occasion and dress the body in the finest clothing. Then a buffalo robe was wrapped about it, and lastly the body placed in buffalo rawhide and securely tied with rawhide ropes, after which it was carried by travois to the foothills or mountains, preferably where the

Burial

bundle could be fastened to the branches of a tree (33)." There was no burial service. The death was announced by the loud weeping and wailing of the women. Occasionally, the warrior's best-loved horse was killed and laid beneath him so that he would have a pony to ride in the land of souls.

An Indian's most sacred possession was his calumet or peace pipe. Without a calumet, no ceremony was effective. It was used in council, at all dance celebrations and other important

The Peace Pipe

occasions. The pipe's greatest significance was as a symbol of peace. According to Chief Standing Bear, "If this sacred symbol was taken to Sioux warriors in the thickest of battle, they would at once obey its mandate and retire (34)." To disobey would bring down disaster upon the head of the warrior and his whole band.

No account of the religious life of the Plains Indians would be complete without a description of their games. Games were opportunities for display and prayer. The young men ran races,

Two Sioux ceremonies *Above* The Dance of the Thunderbirds *Below* The Pony Dance

had archery contests and played team games. One of the most famous was a primitive form of lacrosse. "Each party," wrote George Catlin, "had their goal made with two upright posts, about twenty-five feet high and six apart, set firm in the ground, with a pole across at the top. These goals were about forty or fifty rods apart (35)." They used sticks "bent into an oblong hoop at the end, with a slight web of small thongs tied across, to prevent the ball from passing through (36)." A gun was fired to start the game and "an instant struggle ensued between the players, who were some six or seven hundred in numbers, and were mutually endeavouring to catch the ball in their sticks, and throw it home (37)." Catlin continued, "Hundreds are running together and leaping, actually over each other's heads, and darting between their adversaries legs, tripping and throwing, and foiling each other in every possible manner, and every voice raised to the highest key, in shrill yelps and barks (38)!" The Indians gambled heavily on the outcome of these games and celebrated their conclusion with mugs of whiskey.

Games

Before the outbreak of the Great Indian Wars, the Plains Indians had developed a highly complicated and successful culture of their own. In the years that followed, it was to be put to the sternest of tests.

Above left Mandan Indians painted for a feast
Above right Big Eagle dressed and armed for battle

Opposite Little Wolf (standing) and Dull Knife, Cheyenne chiefs in a white photographer's studio

3 The Great Sioux Wars

BY THE END OF THE CIVIL WAR in 1865, the area between the Missouri and the Rocky Mountains contained 225,000 Indians, 400,000 whites and at least 15,000,000 buffalo. But by 1900 the Indians had been dispersed, the buffalo slaughtered and 1,500,000 whites dominated the area. What brought about these changes?

First of all, there was a land shortage in the eastern states of America. The settlers found the Plains hard to farm but the lush, green lands of Oregon in the Northwest were ideal. Thousands of pioneers made their way across the prairies in great wagon trains. Then, in 1848, gold was discovered in California. Thousands of would-be prospectors moved west to seek their fortunes. *Land shortage*

The Plains Indians regarded the whites with fear and loathing. As they made their way along the famous Santa Fe and Oregon trails, they hunted and killed great numbers of buffalo upon which the Indians depended. As soon as the settlers entered Indian territory, they were followed by bands of Indians waiting for an opportunity to attack the slow-moving wagons. When attacked, "the wagons are drawn into a circle," wrote George Stewart, a pioneer, in 1844. "Around them gallop the Indians on their ponies, shooting arrows. From the shelter of the wagons, the men fire their rifles. Children cower in the wagon boxes, and women crouch with them or load rifles for the men. Indian after Indian tumbles from his pony (39)." Usually, the settlers managed to fight their way through thanks to their superior firepower. *The Wagon Trains*

The American government built and garrisoned a series of

Opposite A wagon train of settlers under attack on the plains

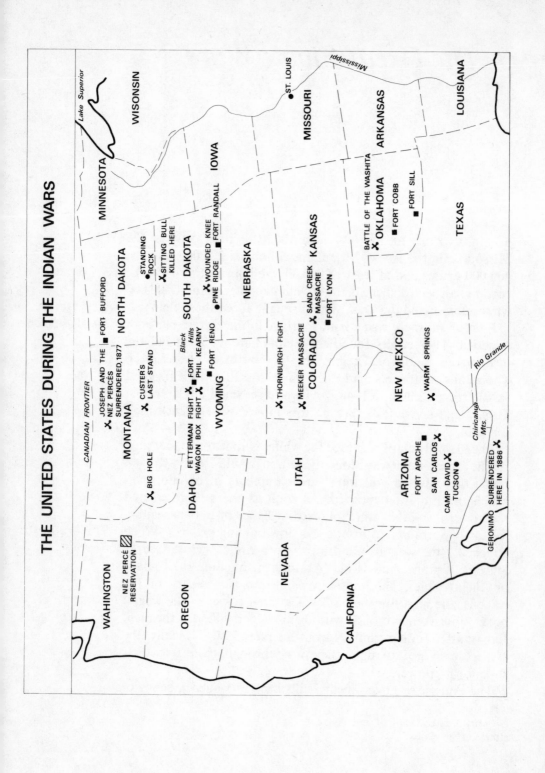

THE UNITED STATES DURING THE INDIAN WARS

forts along the trails to protect the pioneers. They persuaded some of the tribes to enter reservations, but this did not always work out well. For example in 1861 the Cheyenne agreed to retire to a small reservation in southeastern Colorado, but could not find enough game to live on. Some of the braves wandered off the reservation and started rustling cattle. The whites were furious and decided to teach the whole nation a lesson. Colonel John Chivington led the Colorado Volunteers to Fort Lyon where he knew that two peaceful Cheyenne tribes, led by chiefs Black Kettle and White Antelope, had set up their winter camp. As soon as he arrived, he started to plan an attack on the unsuspecting Indians. When some of his officers objected, Chivington roared, "Damn any man who sympathizes with Indians. I have come to kill Indians, and believe it is right and honourable to use any means under God's heaven to kill Indians (40)."

"I have come to kill Indians"

At daybreak on 29th November, 1864, the soldiers attacked. George Bent, a half-breed who was living with the Cheyenne at the time, recalled, "in the camps all was confusion and noise – men, women and children rushing out of the lodges partly dressed; men, women and children screaming at the sight of the troops; men running back into the lodges for their arms (41)." At first, Black Kettle was not unduly worried because he believed that he was under the protection of the Great White Father. He had the Stars and Stripes run up and waited for the soldiers. Almost at once, the troops opened fire and a truly savage battle took place. Robert Bent, another eyewitness, saw "one squaw lying on the bank whose leg had been broken by a shell; a soldier came up to her with a drawn sabre; she raised her arm to protect herself, when he struck, breaking her arm; she rolled over and raised her other arm, when he struck, breaking it, and then left her without killing her (42)." Not even little children were safe. Bent continued, "I saw a little girl about five years of age who had been hid in the sand; two soldiers discovered her, drew their pistols and shot her (43)."

Sand Creek Massacre

Afterwards, Lieutenant James Connor went over the battle-field. "I did not see a body of man, woman, or child but was scalped," he recorded, "and in many instances their bodies were mutilated in the most horrible manner – men, women and children's privates cut out. I heard one man say that he had cut out a woman's private parts and had them for exhibition on a stick; I heard another man say he had cut the fingers off an Indian to get the rings on the hand (44)." Of the 133 Indians killed, 105 were women and children. Chivington reported that he had won "a great victory."

Black Kettle led the survivors through the bitter cold to the camp of the Northern Cheyenne at Smoky Hill. George Bent described the terrible scene at the end of the journey: "Everyone was crying, even the warriors, and the women and children screaming and wailing. Nearly everyone present had lost some relatives or friends, and many of them in their grief were gashing themselves with their knives until the blood flowed in streams (45)." When the news of the Sand Creek Massacre reached the Kiowas, the Arapahoes and the Sioux, they went on the warpath.

Undeterred, in 1866 the government sent Colonel Henry Carrington with 700 men to build a chain of forts along the Bozeman Trail to the newly discovered goldfields in Montana. When Red Cloud, the famous chief of the Oglala Sioux, heard about this, he exclaimed bitterly, "Our women and children will starve, but for my part I prefer to die fighting (46)." Meanwhile, Carrington started to build Fort Phil Kearny. While the soldiers were cutting down trees one day in December, they were attacked by a small band of Indians. A few howitzer shells were enough to disperse the hostile Indians and so Captain William Fetterman rode after them with eighty troopers. The soldiers were ambushed at Peno Creek and massacred.

A year later, Red Cloud attacked another party of wood-cutters, but this time he had an unpleasant surprise. Captain J. N. Powell ordered his men to take the wheels off their wagons and arrange the boxes in a circle. When the Indians attacked the wagons, they were met with a hail of bullets. "It was like green grass withering in a fire," said a warrior called Fire Thunder. "So we picked up our wounded and went away. I do not know how many of our people were killed, but there were very many. It was bad (47)." The soldiers had just been issued with Springfield–Allin repeating rifles. Previously, when the soldiers

Mutilation

"Blood flowed in streams"

Fetterman Massacre

"Green grass withering in a fire"

56

Above The execution of thirty-eight Sioux at Mankato, Minnesota, on Boxing
Day 1862

White settlers defend their home against the Indians

had been armed with single-shot rifles, the Indians had had a good chance of forcing their way into a circle of wagons as soon as the first volley had been fired. That tactic was now a thing of the past.

In spite of this defeat, Red Cloud refused to make peace until the government agreed to abandon the Bozeman Trail. Finally, in 1868, the government gave way and accepted his terms. When the soldiers marched out of Fort Phil Kearny, the jubilant Sioux and Cheyenne set it on fire. In addition, the government promised to keep white settlers out of Indian territory.

1868 Treaty

Meanwhile, Black Kettle and his Cheyenne were in trouble again. Although most of his people had remained peaceful, a few had gone off raiding in Kansas. Remembering what had happened before, Black Kettle asked to be allowed to camp under the walls of Fort Cobb, but permission was refused. At this time, General Philip Sheridan, who was in charge of the Kansas forts, sent Colonel George Custer south to the Washita river to find the winter camp of the hostiles. Custer had orders "to destroy their villages and ponies, to kill or hang all warriors, and to bring back all women and children (48)."

At dawn on 27th November, 1867, Custer's men swept down into Black Kettle's camp. The old chief rode towards the cavalry-men with his hand raised in friendship but was gunned down. Next minute, the soldiers were among the Indians shooting and stabbing. As soon as the warriors rallied, Custer withdrew after killing ninety-two women and children and eleven warriors. When Custer returned with Black Kettle's scalp, General Sheridan was delighted. In his report, Sheridan claimed that the battle of the Washita was caused by the chief, who refused to enter Fort Cobb. Later, he gave it as his opinion that "The only good Indians I ever saw were dead (49)." In due course, this cruel remark became a popular saying: "The only good Indian is a dead Indian."

Battle of the Washita

In the years that followed, President Grant tried to establish better relations with the Indians by seeing that their agencies kept them well supplied with food. Gradually, most of them came to rely upon these supplies in winter, but in spring they set out for their old hunting grounds as usual. However, some of the

General Custer (*left*) and General Sheridan

leading chiefs remained irreconcilable. Among the Sioux, chiefs Sitting Bull, Gall and Crazy Horse refused to change their traditional way of life and ignored the government.

Meanwhile, gold was discovered in the Black Hills of Dakota in 1874 and prospectors swarmed into the territory in spite of the 1868 treaty. General Custer, as he now was, was sent to investigate the prospectors' claims. When he was able to substantiate them, the government decided to buy the Black Hills from the Indians. But the Indians refused to sell even for $6,000,000, for as Chief Crazy Horse put it, "One does not sell the earth upon which the people walk (50)."

Gold in the Black Hills

President Grant ordered the Indians to return to their agencies by 31st January, 1876, or "military force would be sent to compel them (51)." When the couriers reached the Sioux chiefs, it was already winter and too late for them to move. As one Indian put it, "It was very cold and many of our people and ponies would have died in the snow. Also, we were in our own country and were doing no harm (52)." The Army did not accept these arguments. On 17th March General George Crook made a surprise attack on a Sioux village on the Powder River, Montana territory. An Indian called Wooden Leg described what hap-

59

Overleaf The Battle of the Little Bighorn – General 'Long Hair' Custer (centre) fires at the advancing Sioux

pened: "Old people tottered and hobbled away out of reach of the bullets singing among the lodges. Braves seized whatever weapons they had and tried to meet the attack (53)." Most of the women and children escaped up the hillsides while the warriors held the soldiers at bay. Then, the soldiers burned the village. "I had nothing left but the clothing I had on (54)," complained Wooden Leg. But that night, the Indians crept up to the soldiers' camp and recovered their horses, to the fury of General Crook.

It was June before the Army took the field again. It was decided to make a three-pronged attack on the Indians. General Crook advanced up the Bozeman Trail, Colonel John Gibbon marched down the Yellowstone and General Alfred Terry left Fort Lincoln, North Dakota. As Terry approached the Little Bighorn River, his scouts located a great Indian village up ahead. Then he and Gibbon advanced up the Bighorn and sent "Long Hair" Custer on ahead to see that the Indians did not

Below Pioneer settlers in Sioux territory

Opposite Red Cloud, chief of the Oglala Sioux at the Battle of Little Bighorn, in old age

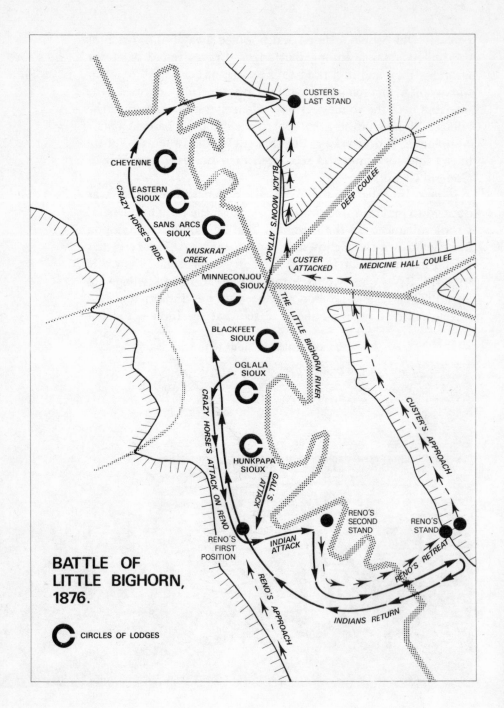

CUSTER'S
LAST STAND

CHEYENNE

EASTERN
SIOUX

CRAZY HORSE'S RIDE

SANS ARCS
SIOUX

DEEP COULEE

BLACK MOON'S ATTACK

MUSKRAT
CREEK

CUSTER
ATTACKED

MEDICINE HALL COULEE

MINNECONJOU
SIOUX

THE LITTLE BIGHORN RIVER

BLACKFEET
SIOUX

OGLALA
SIOUX

CRAZY HORSE'S ATTACK ON RENO

CUSTER'S APPROACH

HUNKPAPA
SIOUX

GALL'S ATTACK

RENO'S
SECOND
STAND

RENO'S
STAND

RENO'S
FIRST
POSITION

INDIAN ATTACK

RENO'S RETREAT

BATTLE OF
LITTLE BIGHORN,
1876.

RENO'S APPROACH

INDIANS RETURN

C CIRCLES OF LODGES

escape. Custer's instructions were none too clear. As he left, General Terry told him, "Use your own judgment, and do what you think best if you strike the trail, and whatever you do, Custer, hold onto your wounded (55)."

Meanwhile, some time before, large numbers of Sioux, Cheyenne and Arapaho had gathered on the Rosebud River in Montana for the annual Sun Dance. Sitting Bull led the dancers. *Rosebud* He had fifty pieces of skin cut from each arm and then started *Dance* to dance in the boiling sun. After a time, he fell into a trance and saw soldiers falling from the sky like grasshoppers. Then, a voice told him, "I give you these because they have no ears (56)." Sitting Bull believed that the Great Spirit had condemned the soldiers to death because they refused to listen to reason. Soon afterwards, the Indians moved their camp to the shore of the Little Bighorn.

General Custer had 31 officers and 585 enlisted men with which to face thousands of Indians. He sent Captain Frederick Benteen with 125 men to scout the hills to the west. Another 130 men were left behind to look after the ammunition train. Major Marcus Reno was ordered to attack the Indian villages in the valley with his 112 troopers while Custer rode along the right bank of the creek with his 225 men.

According to Mrs. Spotted Horn Bull, an eyewitness, "They were six to eight miles distant when first seen . . . We could see the flashing of their sabres and saw that there were very many soldiers in the party (57)." Reno caught the Indians by surprise. "Like that the soldiers were upon us," commented Mrs. Spotted *Battle of the* Horn Bull. "If the soldiers had not fired until all of them were *Little Bighorn* ready for the attack . . . the power of the Dakota nation might have been broken, and our young men killed in the surprise, for they were watching Long Hair only and had no thought of an attack (58)." But as it was, the Indians rallied and hurled themselves on Reno's men. "The air was full of smoke and dust," recalled one of the warriors. "I saw the soldiers fall back and drop into the river bed like buffalo fleeing (59)." Reno made a stand on the bluffs opposite the river. Half his men were dead or wounded when the Indians suddenly dispersed. In fact, they were dashing through the valley to see the death of Custer.

c

Another version of Custer's Last Stand, showing the general impaling an Indian on his sword

Custer rode straight into a trap. Mrs. Spotted Horn Bull was watching. "I knew that the fighting men of the Sioux, many hundreds in number, were hidden in the ravine behind the hill upon which Long Hair was marching, and he would be attacked from both sides (60)." When Custer realized that he was surrounded, he ordered his men to dismount. "They tried to hold onto their horses," remarked Crow King, chief of the Hunkpapa Sioux, "but as we pressed closer they let go their horses. We crowded them towards our main camp and killed them all. They kept in order and fought like brave warriors as long as they had a man left (61)."

No one knows who killed Custer although many warriors claimed the credit. At the end, "He was dressed in buckskin, coat and pants, and was on his hands and knees. He had been

Custer's Last Stand

66

shot through the side, and there was blood coming from his mouth (62)."

Curiously, the Indians did not follow up their victory. They allowed Reno and his battered command to escape and made no attempt to destroy Terry who was still blundering up stream towards them. Instead, they held a great victory celebration and then left. When Terry arrived, he found nothing but the piles of American dead and two magnificent tepees containing eight richly dressed chiefs lying on their burial scaffolds.

When the news reached the East, the public went mad with rage. General Custer and his brave men had been massacred by savages. All Indians must be punished. Congress passed a law taking over the Black Hills and the Powder River country. It was argued that the Indians had broken the 1868 treaty by

making war on the United States. Custer was a hero. A legend
had been born.

Blackfoot scouts on the prairie

4 The Apache Wars

WHILE THE SIOUX were making history at the battle of the Little Bighorn, the Apache were involved in their own life and death struggle with American and Mexican troops. The Apache were mountain Indians occupying parts of Arizona and New Mexico who made a living by hunting and raiding Mexican farms. They had shown little interest in farming since they had been driven up into the mountains by the Spaniards. Because they were used to sudden attacks, they lived in light tepees or "wickey-ups," dome-shaped dwellings made of branches and grasses, which could be easily moved at the first sign of danger. From their earliest years, Apache warriors were subjected to a rigorous training for war. They were made to run for many miles with their mouths full of water, and woe betide the youth who could not spit out the life-giving moisture at the end of his run. To make the young men lithe and quick of movement, they were lined up in front of rocks and shot at with bows and arrows. In this way, the survivors became some of the hardiest and most dangerous warriors that the white man ever had to face. In spite of their ruthless cunning and savage cruelty, the Apache were a free people. Important decisions were made by the tribes as a whole, and not by the chiefs on their own.

A warrior's training

For years the Apache had been on the warpath until their great chief, Mangas Coloradas, attempted to make peace in 1863. He arranged a meeting with General Joseph West of the Californian Volunteers. But as soon as he appeared he was arrested. According to an eyewitness called Daniel Conner, "We hurried Mangas off to our camp at old Fort McClean and arrived in time to see

Katchina dolls representing members of the Hopi tribe performing ceremonial dances

General West come up to his command. The general walked out to where Mangas was in custody to see him, and looked like a pigmy beside the old chief, who towered above everybody about him in stature. He looked careworn and refused to talk and evidently felt that he had made a great mistake in trusting the paleface on this occasion (63)."

Murder General West had the chief put in the guardroom and told the sentries, "I want him dead (64)." Taking him at his word the soldiers heated their bayonets in the fire and placed them on the chief's naked feet until he could bear it no longer. When he rose to complain, "Both sentinels promptly brought down their minie muskets to bear upon him and fired nearly at the same time into his body (65)." Then, they scalped him and cut off his head. The head was boiled until the flesh fell away and was then sold as a souvenir. According to the official report, Mangas was shot while trying to escape. After this murder, there was no chance of peace.

During the next few years, Cochise, the chief of the Chirica- *Cochise* hua Apache, and his lieutenant Geronimo terrorized the valley of the Rio Grande, New Mexico. As the army found it impossible to protect all the settlements from attack, many towns set up their own Committees of Public Safety. In April 1871, the Tucson committee decided to make an example of an Apache village near Camp Grant, Arizona. A band of desperadoes took up position without being seen and opened fire without warning. Many of the Apache panicked and ran into the open where they were shot down. In half an hour, every Apache had been killed or captured or had fled.

When Lieutenant Royal E. Whitman, the commander of the local fort, heard about the attack, he rushed to the scene. "I found quite a number of women shot while asleep beside their bundles of hay which they had collected to bring in that morning," he recalled. "The wounded who were unable to get away had their brains beaten out with clubs or stones, while some *Camp Grant* were shot full of arrows after having been mortally wounded by *Massacre* gunshot. The bodies were all stripped (66)." His surgeon reported that "there can be not doubt that they were first ravished and then shot dead. One infant of some ten months was shot twice and one leg hacked nearly off (67)."

Whitman was so shocked by what he saw that he insisted on those responsible being tried. In spite of the most damning evidence, they were all acquitted and Whitman was hounded out of the Army as an Indian-lover. Nevertheless, this affair drew President Grant's attention to the Southwest and Congress voted seventy thousand dollars "to collect the Apache Indians of Arizona and New Mexico upon reservations . . . and promote peace and civilization among them (68)." General George Crook was sent to carry out these instructions.

At first, Crook tried to capture Cochise and his band in the

71

Overleaf Frederic Remington's famous painting *Dash for Timber* shows a posse of white settlers escaping from the Apache

Frederic Remington's *Signal Fire* shows Indians of the New Mexico desert

mountains, but the wily old chief quickly crossed the border into Mexico. However, he agreed to meet General Oliver Howard, a special peace commissioner, in 1872.

"The Great White Father, President Grant, sent me to make peace between you and the white people," the general told him.

"Nobody wants peace more than I do," replied Cochise.

"Then," said Howard, "we can make peace (69)."

Cochise makes peace

This was easier said than done. Cochise could not see why he and his people should live on a reservation. In the end, he agreed to settle down on part of the Chiricahua Mountains. Howard was a remarkable man and won the trust of the Indians. Geronimo said of him, "He always kept his word with us and treated us as brothers . . . He placed an agent at Apache Pass who issued us from the Government clothing, rations and supplies (70)."

Cochise and his Apaches kept their word and there was peace. Then, in 1874, the great chief was taken seriously ill. As he lay dying, he made his sons promise to honour his treaty with General Howard. Everything remained quiet until 1876 when two white whiskey traders were killed by drunken Chiricahuas. As a result, the whole tribe was ordered to the White Mountain reservation. Most of the Chiricahuas obeyed except for Geronimo and his band who fled to Mexico. For the rest of the year, Geronimo lived by raiding and then joined Chief Victorio and *Geronimo*

Apache women and children in a hut built from leaves and branches

Geronimo, chief of the Apache, under arrest at Fort Pickens, 1886

the Mimbres Apache at the Warm Springs reservation, New Mexico.

John Clum, an Indian agent, was ordered to arrest Geronimo and his men and transfer them to San Carlos in Arizona where they could be tried for robbery and murder. In his autobiography Geronimo described what happened: "Two companies of scouts were sent from San Carlos. They sent word for me and Victorio to come to town. The messengers did not say what they wanted with us, but as they seemed friendly we thought they wanted a council and rode in to meet the officers. As soon as we arrived in town soldiers met us, disarmed us, and took us both to headquarters where we were tried by court-martial. They asked us only a few questions and then Victorio was released and I was sentenced to the guardhouse. Scouts conducted me to the guardhouse and put me in chains. When I asked them why they did this they said it was because I had left Apache Pass (71)."

Arrest

Geronimo did not understand the white man's point of view. "I do not think that I ever belonged to those soldiers at Apache Pass, or that I should have asked them where I might go (72)." He was released four months later. Meanwhile, Victorio and his tribe were transferred to San Carlos. Unfortunately, there was not enough food to go round on the reservation so Victorio and over 300 followers left and took to the mountains. They spent their time raiding ranches in New Mexico and Texas and fighting off the soldiers sent after them. Soon, Victorio became a hardened killer who took a cruel delight in torturing and mutilating his victims. At last, on 14th October, 1880, he and his band were trapped in the Tres Castillos Hills in northern Mexico. Victorio and seventy-eight Apaches were killed in the subsequent battle.

Victorio

As time went by, the Chiricahua Apache on the White Mountain reserve grew more and more restive. When it was

Life on the reservation, 1870

whispered in 1881 that their chiefs were to be arrested, Geronimo and about a hundred Apache fled to Mexico. Encouraged by their success, they returned to the reservation and forced the rest of the tribe to join them. They even managed to defeat six companies of American cavalry who had been sent to cut off their retreat. However, on reaching Mexico, their luck ran out. They blundered into a Mexican infantry regiment and nearly all their women and children were killed before they knew what was happening. Geronimo survived and was more determined than ever to fight to the death.

Geronimo on the Warpath

The government turned to General Crook once more. As soon as he took command of the department of Arizona, he carried out an investigation into the running of the reservation. The results showed, he said, that the Apaches "had not only the best reasons for complaining, but had displayed remarkable forbearance in remaining at peace (73)." Crook ordered all the white squatters and miners off the reservation and told the Indians that they could live wherever they liked on it. Then he slipped across the border and arranged a meeting with Geronimo. The chief agreed to return to the reservation and was escorted back to San Carlos. Unfortunately, General Crook had Geronimo's herd of cattle confiscated and sold. Geronimo was furious. "I told him that these were not white men's cattle, but belonged to us, for we had taken them from the Mexicans during our wars. I also told him that we did not intend to kill these animals, but that we wished to keep them and raise stock on our range. He would not listen to me (74)." The Apache chief knew nothing about the treaties between the United States and Mexico. As far as he was concerned, this was another example of the white man's deceit.

Geronimo surrenders

Nevertheless, all went well for a time. Then the Indians became bored with reservation life. Indeed, there was little for them to do except to draw their rations and drink to excess. Moreover, it was said that Geronimo was to be arrested, so he and several other leaders left the reservation with 34 warriors, 8 boys and 92 women and children. As soon as the newspapers got hold of the story, they predicted that Geronimo would carry fire and devastation throughout the territory. Actually,

Life on the Reservation

78

nothing was further from his mind. He wanted to cross over into Mexico as quickly as possible.

Once again, General Crook refused to be panicked by the trouble makers. He collected a small force and went off to find the old chief. Meanwhile, Geronimo had discovered that the Sierra Madre mountains were no longer a safe haven. The Mexicans sent a large army to exterminate his band. When he met General Crook on 25th March, 1886, Geronimo agreed to surrender. However, on the journey back, Geronimo was told by a renegade American that he was to be hanged as soon as they reached Arizona. The old chief lost his nerve and bolted with 17 warriors, 13 women and 6 children.

Geronimo's Last Campaign

As a result, General Crook was severely censured for his leniency. He resigned and was replaced by General Nelson Miles, a dangerously ambitious man. Five thousand soldiers were occupied trying to track down Geronimo's little band. Geronimo had some close shaves. "One time," he told his biographer, "they surprised us about nine o'clock in the morning and captured all our horses (nineteen in all) and secured our store of dried meats. We also lost three Indians in the encounter. About the middle of the afternoon of the same day we attacked them from the rear as they were going through a prairie – killed one soldier, but lost none ourselves. In this skirmish we recovered all our horses except three that belonged to me (75)."

However, even a leader of Geronimo's undoubted cunning could not hold out indefinitely against overwhelming odds, and so on 3rd September, 1886, he met General Miles at Skeleton Canyon. According to Geronimo, Miles promised, "I will take you under Government protection; I will build you a house; I will fence you much land; I will give you cattle, horses, mules and farming implements (76)." This account has been corroborated by independent witnesses. Then, Geronimo vowed, "I will quit the warpath and live at peace hereafter (77)."

Skeleton Canyon

General Miles' official report is somewhat different: "Geronimo came from his mountain camp amid the rocks and said he was willing to surrender. He was told that they could surrender as prisoners-of-war (78)." It seems that General Miles deliberately misled Geronimo. In fact, the Chiricahuas were sent to

Florida while Geronimo was imprisoned in Fort Pickens, Pensacola. Later, he was released and rejoined his family at Mount Vernon Barracks, Alabama. "We stayed six years (between May 1888 and October 1894) and worked for the Government," said Geronimo. "We had no property, and I looked in vain for General Miles to send me to that land of which he had spoken (79)."

Almost a fourth of the band died in the first three years.
"Dreary monotony of their empty lives" General Crook diagnosed "Homesickness, change of climate, and the dreary monotony of their empty lives (80)" as the main causes. In 1889, Geronimo sent one of his wives with their two children to the Mescalero Indian Agency in New Mexico, even though he knew that this was the last time he would see them. Later, she married again.

In 1894, Geronimo and his people were moved to Fort Sill in Oklahoma, where they were given houses, cattle, hogs, turkeys and chickens. As farmers, they achieved some success although Geronimo later complained that "The Indians did not do much with the hogs, because they did not understand how to care for
"We did better with the turkeys" them, and not many Indians even at the present time [1905] keep hogs. We did better with the turkeys and chickens, but with these we did not have as good luck as white men do. With the cattle we have done very well indeed, and we like to raise them. We have a few horses, also, and have had no bad luck with them (81)."

Geronimo's fame was by this time so great that President Theodore Roosevelt had him ride in his inaugural parade – "I wanted to give the people a good show," remarked the new President. The old chief took the opportunity to ask if he might return home. "Great Father, other Indians have homes where they live and be happy. I and my people have no home . . . Let
"Let me die in my own country" me die in my own country (82)." But there was no mercy for Geronimo; he died a prisoner in 1909. Not until 1913 did the rest of the survivors get the chance to go home. In fact, a third of them chose to remain in Oklahoma where they have given their name to the town of Apache. The rest rejoined the Mescaleros in New Mexico.

5 *The Nez Percé and the Utes*

THE NEZ PERCÉ lived on the Pacific side of the Rocky Mountains in parts of present day Idaho, Washington and Oregon. Almost their first contact with white men had been when Lewis and Clark Clark staggered into their midst on their famous journey to the Pacific in 1805, though they had been given their name by French explorers in the seventeenth century who noticed that they pierced their noses so that they could wear pieces of shell and bone through their septa. However, by the nineteenth century, this custom had virtually died out. *Nez Percé*

The Nez Percé had originally been hunters, fishers and collectors but by the nineteenth century, they had made their name as horsebreeders. The plateau lands they lived on were ideal for horses, which had escaped from Spanish ranches in Mexico, and which gave the Indians a new mobility and enabled them to abandon the agricultural life. Although the summers were hot and dry, the winters were mild and free from snow in the protected river valleys where the Indians lived. *The coming of the horse*

As soon as the Nez Percé obtained horses, they were able to cross the mountains each year to hunt the buffalo. These great animals helped to supplement the meat they obtained from their native elk and deer. The Nez Percé were particularly fortunate in the number of edible roots and bulbs that grew wild in their area. They dug up the sweet tasting bulbs of the Camas, a lily-like plant, and Kouse roots which tasted like turnips. However, it was the coming of the salmon in June that provided them with their major source of food. They caught the great fish in their nets as they swam upriver to spawn. This was a time of great feasting and merrymaking. However, much of the catch was sliced, dried, and kept for the winter when it was carefully cooked in its own oil to make a fairly palatable meal.

The Nez Percé started to dress like the Plains Indians. The men wore breechcloths, leggings, belts, shirts and moccasins, while the women made themselves dresses out of two whole deerskins sewn together. Both sexes wore warm fur hats. They streaked their faces with yellow and red paint and dyed their horses' manes and tails black and red. In summer, they lived in skin tepees but returned to their more substantial longhouses in winter.

By the middle of the nineteenth century, the Nez Percé had become very successful cattlemen as well as horse-breeders, and had built up a flourishing trade with the white communities. However, they already had the reputation of being fierce fighters who followed their chiefs with great loyalty. For fifty years after Lewis and Clark's expedition the only whites to venture west of the Rockies were peaceful hunters and traders, but eventually the settlers of the Plains began to penetrate the mountains. In 1855 and 1863, the Nez Percé sold so much of their land to the whites that they only had a small reservation in Idaho left. Only one Nez Percé chief had refused to sign these treaties.

Old Joseph His name was Old Joseph. As he lay dying, he warned his son Young Joseph, "A few more years and the white man will be all around you. They have their eyes on this land. My son, never forget my dying words. This country holds your father's body. Never sell the bones of your father and mother (83)."

Young Joseph kept his promise to his father. When government officials ordered him to move his people to the Lapwai

"We will defend this land" reservation, he refused and warned them. "We will defend this land as long as a drop of Indian blood warms the hearts of our men (84)." For the time being, the chief's courage was rewarded as President Grant recognized their homelands as a reservation. Unfortunately, not long afterwards, gold was discovered in the nearby mountains and white prospectors poured into their lands.

Under pressure from the whites, the government ordered

Joseph's band to move to the Lapwai reservation in Montana.

The art of the Indians of the North-West: *top left,* soapstone carving of a bear; *top right*, a chief's blanket; *bottom left*, dance apron; *bottom right*, dance mask

Meriwether Lewis and William Clark holding a council with the Indians, 1812

General Oliver Howard was sent out to superintend the operation in 1876. This was the time of the Sioux Wars and Howard feared that the Indians of the northwest would unite. As a result, he only gave Chief Joseph thirty days to move his people to the reservation. "The white men were many and we could not hold our own with them," admitted Chief Joseph. "We were like deer. They were like grizzly bears. We had a small country. Their country was large (85)."

The Nez Percé lost many of their cattle when they tried to cross the swollen rivers. In these circumstances, some of the

young warriors raided a white settlement and got hold of some liquor. Drunk, they lost control and killed fourteen people. In fact, these were the only atrocities committed by the Indians in the so-called Nez Percé War. Fearing the white man's revenge, Chief Joseph, who had been away hunting when the massacre took place, decided to make for Canada. When Howard heard the news, he believed that his worst fears had been realized and set off in hot pursuit.

The Nez Percé took to the mountains and led the American soldiers a merry dance. The Indians fought many successful skirmishes until they reached the Big Hole River. Here, they

paused to rest. During the night of the 9th August, 1877, the soldiers attacked. A fifteen-year-old boy described what happened: "I jumped from my blankets and ran about thirty feet and threw myself on hands and knees, and kept going. An old woman, Patsikonmi, came from the tepee and did the same thing . . . She was to my left and was shot in the breast. I heard the bullet strike. She said to me, 'You better not stay here. Be going. I'm shot.' Then she died. Of course I ran for my life and hid in the bushes. The soldiers seemed shooting everywhere. Through tepees and wherever they saw Indians. I saw little children and men fall before bullets coming like rain (86)." Two-thirds of the eighty Indians killed were women and children. The Nez Percé fought back bravely but were forced to withdraw.

"We retreated as rapidly as we could," recalled Chief Joseph. "After six days General Howard came close to us and we went out and attacked him, and captured nearly all the horses and mules (87)." Without his pack animals, Howard was forced to move more slowly and it seemed as if the Nez Percé would escape. But, while they were crossing Yellowstone Park, they were sighted by the Seventh Cavalry, who were burning to avenge their defeat at the Little Bighorn. From that moment onwards, the Indians received no peace. There was fighting between them and the cavalry almost daily.

The Seventh Cavalry

When they were within a few miles of the Canadian border, the Nez Percé fought their last savage battle. "We fought at close range," said Chief Joseph, "not more than twenty steps apart, and drove the soldiers back upon their main line, leaving their dead in our hands. We secured their arms and ammunition (88)." In spite of this victory, the Nez Percé were exhausted. When General Miles, the commander of the cavalry, asked Chief Joseph to meet him and discuss the situation, he had to agree, but when the chief appeared in front of the general's tent under a flag of truce, he was seized and placed under arrest. In retaliation, the Nez Percé captured one of the general's staff and threatened to kill him unless Joseph was released. The chief was set free and returned to his people.

Meanwhile, General Howard arrived with reinforcements. Joseph knew now that he was beaten. He called a council and addressed his people. "I am tired of fighting," he told them.

85

A wagon train bound for the Oregon coast attacked by the Nez Percé

"Our chiefs are killed . . . The old men are dead . . . It is cold and we have no blankets. The little children are freezing to death . . . Hear me, my chiefs! I am tired; my heart is sick and sad. From where the sun now stands I will fight no more forever (89)." Weeping, the chiefs agreed. They had marched 1,300 miles through the mountains of Idaho, Wyoming and Montana; all to no avail.

Chief Joseph and his followers were sent to Fort Leavenworth in Kansas. The chief was naturally bitter. "General Miles promised that we might return to our own country," he claimed. "I believed General Miles, or I never would have surrendered (90)." However, General Miles was not to blame. He had been overruled by the War Department and there was nothing he could do about it. Many of the Nez Percé learned to farm and were allowed to return to their homelands in 1885. Chief Joseph, however, spent the rest of his life on the Colville reserva-

86

Opposite 'Young' Joseph, chief of the Nez Percé, in ceremonial dress

tion in Washington where he died in 1904.

The Utes, too, lived in the Rocky Mountains. In the second half of the nineteenth century, there were some 3,500 of them, forming six loosely organized bands. For many years, they had raided the weaker tribes to the south and been preyed upon by the more powerful Cheyennes and Arapahos. Originally, they had scraped a bare living as hunters, collecters and fishermen, but, like the Nez Percé, their lives had been transformed by the coming of the horse. They too made the great trek across the mountains to the high plains to hunt the buffalo. At home, they organized great antelope-hunts. They drove the terrified beasts into corrals made of bush and slaughtered them, gorging themselves on the red meat. In addition, their women scoured the countryside for edible fruits, roots and bulbs. They too relied upon large catches of fish which were trapped in great nets, eight by thirty feet in size.

The Utes

Their contact with the Sioux and Cheyennes had a deep and abiding influence, especially upon their religious life. The Sun Dance became their most important ceremony although they added their own interpretation. For example, all the Ute warriors and women danced opposite each other instead of confining the ceremony to a few chosen individuals.

By the 1860s, the Utes were particularly fine horsemen and fierce warriors. For this reason and because they hated the Plains Indians with whom they had clashed so frequently, the Utes were employed as mercenaries by the United States army. Many of their warriors served with distinction in the campaigns against the Comanche and Navajo nations. Even when the first settlers moved into their tribal lands, the Utes accepted the white man without fear. In 1863, they signed away all of Colorado east of the Continental Divide. In return, they were promised $20,000 worth of goods and supplies each year for ten years. By 1868, land was in such great demand that the Ute chiefs were invited to visit the Federal capital, Washington D.C. The leader of the Utes was Ouray, a very intelligent Indian who spoke English. He realized at once what the government wanted, but as he said, "The agreement an Indian makes to a United States treaty is like the agreement a buffalo makes with his hunters

Joining the U.S. Army

when pierced with arrows. All he can do is lie down and give in (91)." As a result of the new treaty, two agencies were set up at Los Pinos and White River, Montana.

However, it soon became clear that the Coloradans would not be satisfied until every Ute had been driven out of the territory. Even the governor was elected on a "Utes Must Go" platform. Moreover, in 1878, a meddler called Nathan C. Meeker arrived at White River as agent. He was determined to civilize the Utes and turn them into farmers. To that end, he set up a model farm. In spite of all his efforts, the Utes took no notice of his project. The angry agent decided to use force and ordered his men to start ploughing up the Utes' grazing land.

"The Utes must go"

When an Indian called Johnson complained that he needed the pasture for his horses, Meeker replied, "The trouble is, Johnson, you have too many ponies. You had better kill some of them! (92)." The Indian was so angry that he could not trust himself to speak, but pushed past Meeker and stalked away. Meeker was beside himself with rage and sent for Nicaagat, the local chief, and told him that he was going to ask the Commissioner of Indian Affairs for soldiers to drive the Utes from their lands.

"You have too many ponies"

As he threatened, Meeker wrote to the Commissioner, claiming: "I have been assaulted by a leading chief, Johnson, forced out of my house and injured badly (93)." He asked for military protection. As a result, the Commissioner ordered Meeker to arrest the leaders of the "disturbance." Troops were sent from Fort Fred Steele under Major Thomas Thornburgh to help him. When Chief Nicaagat heard of their approach, he rode out to meet with the Major to try to stop him. However, Thornburgh insisted that he could only change his plans if Meeker required it. The chief went back to the agent and warned him that his followers would regard the advance of Thornburgh's troops as a declaration of war. Realizing, at last, the full danger of the situation, Meeker sent off the necessary message to the major. Unfortunately, Thornburgh decided that he would have to enter the reservation to make sure that he could reach the agency should it be attacked.

Major Thornburgh

As Thornburgh's column passed through the reservation

Berries being dried for winter food by Indians of the North-West

Chief Nicaagat rode out again to meet him. "As soon as they saw me," claimed the chief, "they deployed off one after another. I was with General Crook the year before, fighting the Sioux, and I knew in a minute that as soon as this officer deployed his men out in that way it meant fight (94)." Nevertheless, he carried

A settler's house in the Rocky Mountains attacked by Indians

on towards Thornburgh until a shot was fired. "In a second so many shots were fired," Nicaagat continued, "that I knew I could not stop the fight, although I swung my hat to my men and shouted, 'Don't fire, we only want to talk.' But they understood me to be encouraging them to fight (95)."

The Meeker Massacre

After the battle started, a band of Indians rode over to the agency and killed Meeker and his workmen. The three white women at the post were captured, raped and carried off. The fighting continued for about a week and Thornburgh and twelve soldiers were killed and another forty-three wounded. The Utes lost thirty-seven warriors.

When Chief Ouray heard the news, he sent off a message to all Utes: "You are hereby requested and commanded to cease hostilities against the whites (96)." But it was already too late, the damage had been done. The newspapers flooded the territory with lurid atrocity stories and the governor insisted that "unless [the Utes] are removed by the government, they must necessarily

Punishment

be exterminated." He went on, "I could raise 25,000 men to protect the settlers in twenty-four hours. The state would be willing to settle the Indian trouble at its own expense. The advantage that would accrue from throwing open 12,000,000 acres of land to miners and settlers would more than compensate all the expenses incurred (97)."

In the event, the Utes released the white women and laid down their arms, but it made no difference. The Commission of Inquiry decided that they had ambushed the soldiers and massacred the civilians. Chief Ouray went to Washington in 1880 to plead for his people, but it was already too late. The Indian Bureau had decided to remove the Utes to a new reservation in Utah. Chief Ouray did not live to see the final humiliation of his people in 1881. With the Utes gone, the whole of Colorado belonged to the white man.

6 The Ghost Dance

THE SIOUX TRIUMPH after the battle of the Little Bighorn was short-lived. The soldiers surrounded the Powder River country in Montana and destroyed the Indians' winter camps. For example, General Crook stumbled upon Chief American Horse's village in a canyon near Slim Buttes. When the firing started *Fight at* American Horse ordered his people to escape into the hills *Slim Buttes* while he hid in a cave and kept the soldiers at bay for as long as he could. After several hours of fierce fighting American Horse surrendered. He emerged from his cave holding his entrails in his hands. Since there was nothing that could be done for his shattered body, he sat down by the fire and calmly waited to die.

Most of the Sioux bands surrendered and settled around the agency buildings on their reservations. However, a die-hard minority led by Chiefs Sitting Bull and Gall moved north and *Sitting Bull* crossed into Canada in December 1876. The American govern- *and Gall* ment was furious and the Canadian authorities deeply embarrassed. Canada had her own Indian problems. There was hardly enough game to keep the native Indians alive, let alone the newcomers. In these circumstances, Sitting Bull and the other chiefs agreed to meet American peace commissioners at Fort Walsh.

With singular lack of tact, the government made General Terry leader of the Commission. Only the previous year, he had been doing his best to exterminate the Sioux. Not surprisingly, harsh words were spoken on both sides. A squaw spoke for all the Indians when she said, "I came over to this country to raise my children and have a little peace. That is all I have to say to

you. I want you to go back where you came from. These [the Canadians] are the people that I am going to stay with, and raise my children with (98)." When Terry returned to America, he felt that "The presence of this large body of Indians bitterly hostile to us, in close proximity to the frontier, is a standing menace to the peace of our Indian territories (99)."

However, he need not have worried because the Sioux soon found that Canada was not the promised land they had hoped for. The Canadian government could not give them a reservation, nor all the supplies they desperately needed. Their condition steadily deteriorated until by 1881 they were starving. At last, Sitting Bull was forced to face reality and led his people back into the United States. He surrendered to the commander of Fort Buford, North Dakota. Although he was promised that he would not be separated from his people, he was arrested and imprisoned in Fort Randall, until May, 1883. After his release he joined his people on the Standing Rock reservation in North Dakota, where he was closely watched by the agent, James McLaughlin.

Although he remained as defiant as ever, Sitting Bull had become something of a public hero. In 1883, he was invited to the opening of the Northern Pacific Railroad. When it was his turn to speak, he said, "I hate all white people. You are thieves and liars. You have taken away our land and made us outcasts (100)." Fortunately, as he spoke in Sioux, only the official interpreter understood what he said and he calmly read out the official speech as if nothing had happened. The old chief thoroughly enjoyed the rapturous applause with which his insults were received.

"I hate all white people"

Sitting Bull was invited to many more celebrations and visited fifteen cities in 1884. He even joined "Buffalo Bill" Cody's Wild West Show and toured the country until it went on a European visit. At this point, he insisted on returning to his own people. Certainly, his presence was needed, since things were going badly wrong on the reservation. In 1889, America suffered the worst drought on record and the Indians' crops failed completely. To add to their misery, a measles epidemic wiped out hundreds of their children. In the midst of these disasters, news arrived of

Buffalo Bill

95

Opposite 'Buffalo Bill' Cody with Indian chiefs at Pine Ridge, South Dakota

a new messiah who said that the day of the white man was nearly over.

This prophet was a Paiute called Wovoka who lived in the Nevada desert. He claimed that he was Christ reborn as an Indian. "My children," he told the Indians, "I want you to listen to all I have to say to you. I will teach you how to dance a dance, and I want you all to dance it (101)." The Ghost Dance, as it came to be called, spread like wildfire. When Sitting Bull heard about it, he asked McLaughlin if he could visit one of the centres of the new religion to study it but the agent refused to let him go. However, a Sioux medicine man called Kicking Bear came to the Standing Rock agency and initiated Sitting Bull into its mysteries.

The Ghost Dance

Kicking Bear told the Sioux that the Great Spirit had told him, "I will cover the earth with new soil to a depth of five times the height of man, and under this new soil will be buried the whites . . . The new lands will be covered with sweet grass and running water and trees, and herds of buffalo and ponies will stray over it, that my red children may eat and drink, hunt and rejoice . . . And while I am making the new earth the Indians who have heard this message and who dance and pray and believe will be taken up in the air and suspended there, while the wave of new earth is passing; then set down among the ghosts of their ancestors, relatives and friends . . . and while my children are dancing and making ready to join the ghosts, they shall have no fear of the white man, for I will take from the whites the secret of making gunpowder, and the powder they have now will not burn when it is directed against the red people . . . Go then, my children, and tell these things to all the people and make ready for the coming of the ghosts (102)."

Kicking Bear

Sitting Bull quickly accepted the new faith. When the worried Indian agent visited his camp, he found the dance in full swing. "The dancers held each other's hands, and were all jumping madly, whirling to the left about the pole, keeping time to a mournful crooning song, that sometimes rose to a shriek as the women gave way to the stress of their feelings . . . Some of the dancers had thrown off their upper clothing, and all were gasping excitedly; a few who had been dancing for a considerable

Sitting Bull dances

96

Opposite Wovoka, the Paiute Messiah (left),
in 1926, with T. J. McCoy, the white actor

length of time were completely crazed, with their tongues lolling out from their mouths (103)."

When Sitting Bull announced that he was leaving the reservation, McLaughlin ordered his arrest. At first light on 15th December, 1890, forty-three Indian police led by Lieutenant Bull Head and Sergeant Shave Head surrounded Sitting Bull's cabin. Lieutenant Bull Head went in and shook the old man.

"What do you want here?" asked the sleepy chief.

"You are under arrest and must go to the agency," said Bull Head.

"Very well," agreed Sitting Bull, "I will go with you (104)."

By the time he had dressed, a large crowd had collected outside his cabin. When he emerged, his son, Crow Foot, yelled, "You call yourself a brave man and you have declared that you would never surrender to a blue-coat, and now you give yourself up to Indians in blue uniforms (105)!" This taunt hit Sitting Bull hard and he decided to try to escape. He screamed an order to the waiting Indians. Instantly, they opened fire hitting the lieutenant and the sergeant. According to McLaughlin, Bull Head "shot Sitting Bull through the body, and at the same instant Second Sergeant Red Tomahawk, who with revolver in hand was rear-guard, shot him in the right cheek, killing him instantly (106)." Seven more Indians were killed and three wounded in the fighting that ensued. The police had four men killed and another wounded before a detachment of cavalry arrived and rescued them.

Death of Sitting Bull

Ironically, the Sioux's belief in their new religion stopped them rising in revolt after Sitting Bull's death. Instead, several hundred warriors fled to Ghost Dance settlements in other reservations. Some thirty-eight frightened and half frozen Indians joined Chief Big Foot's followers on the Cheyenne River reservation. When he heard what had happened, Big Foot decided to take his people to the Pine Ridge agency for safety. At Wounded Knee Creek, South Dakota, on 28th December, his band was surrounded by a detachment of cavalry and forced to surrender. Shortly afterwards, Colonel James W. Forsyth arrived and took command. He allowed the Indians to make camp and placed his four Hotchkiss guns on a rise overlooking

99

Opposite Chief Gall, a leader of the Ghost Dance movement (for Sitting Bull, see *Frontispiece*)
Overleaf Sitting Bull lies dead on the ground left as the hostile Sioux fight the Indian Police (*Note:* the artist has made a mistake – there were no cannon used in this skirmish)

Top The camp of the hostile Indians before Wounded Knee, at Pine Ridge, South Dakota

Above Big Foot lies dying on the battlefield at Wounded Knee

The Sioux and Cheyenne chief's who negotiated with General Miles and ended the Indian Wars

the tepees.

Foolishly, Forsyth decided to disarm the Indians on the spot. He ordered them to lay down their arms. "So all of us gave the guns and they were stacked up in the centre [of the semi-circle in front of Forsyth's tent] (107)," recalled White Lance. After the soldiers had searched the tepees they approached the Indians. Unfortunately, a brave called Black Coyote had just bought himself a new Winchester rifle and did not want to hand it over. He jumped up and started waving his rifle around. Suddenly, a shot rang out and an officer fell. As the rest of the warriors rose to their feet, they were cut down by a hail of rifle bullets and Hotchkiss shells. Fifty-two Indians were killed by this first volley. "We tried to run," recalled Louise Weasel Bear, "but they shot us like we were buffalo. I know there are some good white people, but the soldiers must be mean to shoot children and women. Indian soldiers would not do that to white children (108)."

The maddened braves fought the soldiers with their knives, clubs and bare hands and then tried to escape up a dry ravine. The bodies of the dead and dying were found strewn over the snow for a distance of three miles. When the fighting was over,

Massacre at Wounded Knee

"They shot us like we were buffalo"

103

the soldiers counted the dead. There were 84 warriors including Big Foot, 44 women and 18 children. At least 33 more were wounded, some of whom died later. Mysteriously, the soldiers suffered 60 casualties: 25 dead and 35 wounded. It seems that many of them were caught in their own crossfire.

When the sound of the shooting reached the agency, some of the warriors leaped onto their horses and rode to Wounded Knee to see what was happening. When they returned with the news, the rest of the Indians panicked. Braves ran about knocking down their tepees and collecting their most prized possessions before making off into the Badlands of South Dakota. By the time the cavalry reached the agency, four out of six thousand Indians had fled. As soon as General Nelson Miles learned of the tragedy, he went to Pine Ridge and took command. The Badlands were surrounded with 8,000 troops. Then, Miles sent messages to the Indians promising them food and peace if they surrendered. The Indians were hungry and outnumbered. They surrendered.

The flight of the Sioux

The massacre at Wounded Knee brought the Great Indian Wars to an end. The Ghost Dance was finished; the heroes of old had not come alive; the whites had not been destroyed. There was no sign of the new earth. All but a few die-hards had to admit that the messiah had been wrong. The good old days were gone for ever, and the Indians would never again wander freely over the plains. The reservation became their home.

End of the Wars

7 *The Indian in Modern America*

FREED FROM THE FEAR of an Indian attack, there was a gradual change in American opinion. Interested people formed the National Indian Association in 1885 and bombarded Washington with petitions calling for better treatment for Indians everywhere. The Indian Rights Association was founded in 1882 and won considerable support by publishing on-the-spot reports on conditions in the reservations. Unfortunately, much of the trouble arose from corruption within the Indian Service. Agents could and did make fortunes out of misappropriating stores and funds intended for the Indians.

Indian Rights Association

Very little effort was made to convert the Indians to Christianity. Although the Christian Churches spent millions of dollars on missions to China, they allocated less than $10,000 annually to the Indians. When missionaries did appear on the reservations, they often quarrelled among themselves. As Chief Joseph of the Nez Percé remarked, "They will teach us to quarrel about God as the Catholics and Protestants do on the reservation. We may quarrel with men sometimes about things on this earth, but we never quarrel about God. We do not want to learn that (109)."

"We never quarrel about God"

Nor were the first efforts to educate the Indians any more successful. This was hardly surprising, as the Agency schools were short of money, and made no effort to interest the children, teaching the same subjects and using the same methods as the white schools. Gradually the Federal government increased its grants, so that by 1899 there were 148 boarding and 225 day schools, educating nearly 20,000 Indian pupils. Unfortunately,

Schools

Taos Pueblo, New Mexico – the inhabitants of this 16th-century village have accepted the Spanish innovation of doors rather than holes in the roof, but refuse electricity and sewers

the education they provided had little practical value for the kind of life that the Indians were condemned to live on the reservation.

In an effort to lessen the tension existing between the Indian agents and their people, Indian police were employed. This was not a new idea, but it received official support in 1878. Unhappily, they were expected to adopt the white man's ways and wear western clothes, cut their hair short and take only one wife at a time. Their own people regarded them as renegades. Moreover, the Courts of Indian Offenses tried to stamp out polygamy, dancing and magic. This made them very unpopular and they had little success.

"Severalty" was another attempt to solve the Indian problem. By an act of 1887, it became possible to break up the reservations *Severalty* and divide them into allotments. This proved to be a bad mistake. Much of the land was unsuitable for agriculture and few Indians made good farmers. Many of them tried to sell their holdings.

When the United States entered the First World War, many *First World* Indians volunteered to serve in the armed forces. In recognition *War* of their public spirited action, American citizenship was granted to all Indians in 1924. However, as Chief Standing Bear pointed

Opposite A school on the Navajo reservation in Arizona

Above A few of the Navajo have found skilled jobs in a uranium mine

Mexican Indian market-traders eating in the streets

Julia Wades-in-the-water retains her traditional dress and *calumet* on a Blackfoot reservation

out in 1931, "The reservation still remains, the agent is still on the job, Indian children are still wrested from their mothers' arms to be sent away, young 'citizens' still go to segregated schools (110)."

For a time in the 1920s, it looked as if the Indians would become extinct like the buffalo, since their death rate far exceeded their birth rate. Then, in 1934, their hopes were raised by the Indian Reorganization Act. This prohibited any further allotment of land and made two million dollars available each year for the acquisition of land for the Indians. The number of boarding schools was drastically reduced and the first contracts were made with state departments of education to enable Indian children to attend state schools. Books on Indian history and culture were produced and Indian children were no longer required to attend church services.

This "Indian New Deal" aroused bitter opposition among the Christian missions. Some super-patriots even believed that it was part of a Communist plot. Nevertheless, under the terms of the Act, 95 tribes became self-governing societies and 74

The Indian New Deal

Navajo Indians queue to vote for their tribal council

formed corporations to conduct their own business. The progress made by these bodies has been uneven. Some have succeeded beyond all expectation, others have completely failed. Belatedly, in 1946, Congress created the Indian Claims Commission to arbitrate upon Indian petitions. However, by the end of the Second World War (1945), this reform drive had burned itself out and the government's attitude was hardening.

With the appointment of Dillon Myer as Commissioner of Indian Affairs in 1950, the development schemes were abandoned. White farmers and businessmen again began to cast greedy eyes toward the Indian lands. In 1953, a law was passed giving *Termination* the states the power to extend their control over the Indian *policy* reservations. Not until 1968 did President Lyndon Johnson pass another bill requiring them to obtain the Indians' permission first! By that time, 61 tribes had lost their federal support. Many Indians sold their allotted land. As one Blackfoot woman 110 explained, "We had to sell our land to live (111)." Many Indians

The exploitation of the Indian – many reservation-dwellers only survive by dressing up and selling their photographs to white tourists made their way to great cities like Chicago, Denver and Los Angeles. In 1956, the Indian Bureau helped no less than 12,626 Indians to go to the cities. A few prospered and settled down, many returned home.

John
F. Kennedy

The 1960 election saw both political parties trying to win the Indian vote. John F. Kennedy promised, "There would be no change in treaty or contractual relationships without the consent of the tribes concerned. No steps would be taken to impair the cultural heritage of any group (112)." Under his administration, help was given to those Indians – some 40% of their population – who had gone to live in the cities. However, of late the difficulties of the American Indians have been pushed into the background by more immediate problems.

The condition of the Indian in America today differs from one tribe to another. Some reservation Indians, like the Navajos, receive healthy incomes from the leasing of mineral deposits found on their land. Others, like the Oklahoma Indians, have organized themselves with considerable success. Most however, are underprivileged citizens who feel that they are ignored by

Red Power

the Federal government. As a result, a Red Power Movement has developed with groups of angry and politically conscious Indians adopting a policy of direct action to bring their case to the attention of the American public.

One such group seized the Island of Alcatraz, the old prison site in San Francisco Bay, in November, 1969. They occupied it in spite of government orders until they were forcibly evicted in June, 1971. In their bitterness, the Indians published a statement explaining why from the white man's viewpoint Alcatraz would have been such a suitable choice for a reservation (113):

1. It is isolated from modern facilities, and without adequate means of transportation.
2. It has no fresh running water.
3. It has inadequate sanitation facilities.
4. There are no oil or mineral rights.
5. There is no industry and so unemployment is very great.
6. There are no health care facilities.
7. The soil is rocky and non-productive, and the land does not support game.

8. There are no education facilities.
9. The population has always exceeded the land base.
10. The population has always been held as prisoners and kept dependent upon others.

This same anger led to some two thousand members of the American Indian Movement (AIM) assembling in Washington on 30 October, 1972. These representatives from two hundred and fifty tribes demanded the reorganization of the Bureau of Indian Affairs and the strict observance of all the existing treaties, some 371 in number, between the United States Government and the Indian tribes. On finding that no arrangements had been made to accommodate them, five hundred Indians, led by Mr Russell Means and Mr Dennis Banks, occupied the Bureau's offices between 2nd and 8th November. When the Indians withdrew, they took with them documents which, they claimed, contained "highly incriminating evidence against ex-Senators and Congressmen from Western States (114)."

Excitement mounted when an Oglala Sioux Indian was killed in a fight with a white man on 21st January 1973. Mr Banks called for a "national day of Indian Rights." Many Indians responded and made their way to the little town of Custer, South Dakota, where the alleged murderer was to receive a preliminary court hearing. To the fury of the Indians, the accused man was only charged with second degree murder and was released on bail. When Mr Banks and Mr Means rose and demanded that the charge be changed to one of first degree murder, fighting broke out between their supporters and the local police. During the subsequent rioting, the nearby Chamber of Commerce was burnt down and the courthouse badly damaged.

Worse was to follow as a result of a quarrel which took place between members of the Oglala Sioux tribal council on the Pine Ridge Reservation. Angry councillors accused their president, Mr Richard Wilson, of misgovernment, misuse of tribal funds and replacing full-blood Indian officials with half-breeds. On failing to obtain his resignation, his opponents asked the American Indian Movement for its help. As a result, it was decided to seize and occupy the hamlet of Wounded Knee. A band of about two hundred Sioux and AIM members took over

The image of the Indian – many white Americans only know the native people through the parodies shown in Hollywood Westerns such as *Finger on the Trigger*

Red Power – a Blackfoot girl stands inside Alcatraz during the Indian occupation of the old Federal prison

the hamlet on 27th February, helped themselves to arms and ammunition, and captured ten hostages including a priest. The hamlet was immediately surrounded by State police and Federal Bureau of Investigation agents.

The Indians demanded that the Senate should investigate the treatment of the Oglala Sioux by the Bureau of Indian Affairs and look into the whole field of relations between the Indians and the Federal Government. Mr Carter Camp, the national co-ordinator of the American Indian Movement, told the authorities that the hostages were in no danger as long as the police kept their distance. But, he warned, "If they [the police] *"If they* come in shooting, its going to be pretty hard to distinguish *come in* between Indians and white people. There is a definite threat of *shooting . . ."* another massacre (115)." Fortunately, this gloomy prophecy was not fulfilled. The Indians and Federal marshals exchanged shots but few people were hurt until 26th March when a Federal marshal was seriously wounded.

After prolonged negotiations, the Indians agreed on 5th April to lay down their arms, but unfortunately due to a mis-understanding over the actual date of their withdrawal, the shooting started again on 17th April. During the next couple of

115

weeks one Indian was fatally wounded and another killed outright. Finally, on 6th May, the Indians agreed to surrender their arms and evacuate Wounded Knee if their leaders could discuss their grievances with representatives of President Nixon.

As a result, Sioux elders from eight reservations and members of the AIM met White House representatives at Kyle, South Dakota, on 17–18 May. The Indians demanded that the Federal

The 1868 treaty

government enforce their 1868 treaty with the Sioux. They pointed out that at the time of the treaty, the Sioux held some 130,000,000 acres of land, and that this had been reduced to 6,900,000 acres over the years. In fact, since 1923 the Sioux have been fighting a legal battle to get these lands back. The Indians also demanded that referenda be held in every reservation to decide whether the Indians wished to continue with the present system of government by tribal councils and presidents or whether they would prefer to return to traditional forms of government.

Mr Leonard Garment, President Nixon's counsel, rejected the demand for the implementation of the 1868 treaty on 31st May, but agreed that the Sioux could do away with their tribal council if the majority of the Indians on the reservation agreed. Quite obviously, this is not the end of the matter. The struggle for what the Indians consider to be their rights will continue for some considerable time. The seizure of Wounded Knee drew attention to the Indians' plight. More than forty per cent of them were unemployed at the time of the siege, which was ten times the national average. Nearly half the population of Indian school-children "dropped out" before obtaining any qualifications.

The actions and claims of these Indians have made all Americans search their consciences, for as Vine Deloria, one

"What is the value of a man's life?"

of the "New Indians", wrote in 1971, "It isn't important that there are only 500,000 of us Indians . . . What is the value of a man's life? That is the question (116)."

Indians claim Italy by right of discovery

From Our Correspondent
Rome, Sept 24

Italy, cradle of Western civilization, woke up today to the fact that it has never actually been discovered. The situation, however, was remedied at 11 o'clock in the morning when the chief of the Indian Chippawa tribe, Adam Nordwall, stepped off an Alitalia jumbo jet and claimed it for the Indian people.

The intrepid explorer, in full Indian dress, accompanied by his wife—in ordinary clothes because her suitcase had been lost in New York—stood on the tarmac of Fiumicino airport here and took possession of Italy "by right of discovery".

The fact that Italy has long been inhabited by people who consider themselves to be in full possession of the place was exactly the point that Mr Nordwall was trying to make. "What right had Columbus to discover America when it was already inhabited for thousands of years? The same right that I have to come now to Italy and claim to have discovered your country", he said.

The difference, however, was that Columbus "came to conquer a country by force where a peaceful people were living, while I am on a mission of peace and goodwill".

Mr Nordwall led a party of Indians which occupied the prison on Alcatraz in San Francisco Bay in 1969 to call attention to the conditions in which Indians were compelled to live in America.

Militant Indians are now (1973) trying to draw the attention of the rest of the world to the situation of their people

117

Table of Dates

20,000 B.C.	Mongoloid people start to cross over the Bering Straits to North America.
1492	Christopher Columbus arrived in the West Indies.
1519–21	Hernando Cortes conquers the Aztecs in Central America.
1521	Ponce de Leon is mortally wounded by the Florida Indians.
1538–42	Hernando de Soto's expedition crosses the Mississippi and explores Arizona, New Mexico, Texas and Kansas.
1607	The English found Jamestown, Virginia.
1620	The Pilgrim Fathers sail to New England.
1672–6	King Philip's War ends the resistance of the tribes of the northeast.
1689–97	King William's War.
1701–13	Queen Anne's War.
1744–48	King George's War.
1756–63	The Seven Years' War: the British defeat the French and take over Canada.
1763	Pontiac's Rising; as a result of this the British tried to stop the colonists from settling in the Ohio Valley.
1775–83	The American War of Independence.
1803	The United States made the Louisiana purchase.
1804–6	Lewis and Clark's expedition to the Pacific.
1824	The Bureau of Indian Affairs set up.
1830	The Removal Bill: President Andrew Jackson hoped to move the eastern Indians across the Mississippi.
1848	Gold is discovered in California causing many thousands to cross over Indian territory in Arizona, New Mexico and California in wagon trains.
1861–65	Civil War.

1863	The Apache leader, Mangas Coloradas, is murdered. The Bozeman Trail to the Montana gold fields is opened and causes trouble among the Sioux.
1864	The Sand Creek Massacre (28th November): Colonel John Chivington and the Colorado Volunteers massacre friendly Cheyennes. This leads to widespread fighting among the Plains Indians.
1866	Colonel Henry Carrington sets out to build a series of forts along the Bozeman trail. Red Cloud and the Sioux go on the warpath. The Fetterman Massacre (21st December).
1867	The Wagon Box Fight: Red Cloud's Sioux are driven off by troops using the new repeating rifles.
1868	The U.S. government closes the Bozeman Trail and ends the Sioux War.
1871	The Camp Grant Massacre: the people of Tucson destroy an Apache village.
1872	Cochise, Chief of the Chiricahua Apache, makes peace with General Oliver Howard.
1874	Custer explores the Black Hills of Dakota and confirms the presence of gold deposits.
1875	President Grant orders the Sioux back onto their reservations.
1876	The battle of Little Bighorn (26th June): Custer and his detachment of the Seventh Cavalry are massacred. Sitting Bull leads his people into Canada.
1877	Chief Joseph leads the Nez Percé rising; gets to within thirty miles of the Canadian frontier before surrendering.
1878	Congress appropriates first funds for the Indian Police.
1880	Chief Victorio of the Mimbres Apache is killed at the battle of Chihuahua.
1881	Sitting Bull leads his people back to America and

	surrenders.
1882	Indian Rights Association is founded.
1883	Courts of Indian Offenses set up.
1885	The last great buffalo herd is destroyed.
1886	Geronimo surrenders and brings the Apache Wars to an end.
1887	The Severalty Act: the reservations could be divided up into allotments.
1889–91	The Ghost Dance Movement: the Indians believe that the Great Spirit is going to destroy the white man.
1890	Sitting Bull is killed while resisting arrest (15th December). The Sioux flee from the soldiers. A group of Sioux are massacred at Wounded Knee Creek (28th December).
1914–18	First World War: Indians volunteer for service in the armed forces.
1924	Congress grants American citizenship to all Indians.
1934	The Indian Reorganization Act gave the Indians a new deal which stopped the sale of tribal lands and made funds available for the purchase of new lands.
1939–45	25,000 Indians are called up and serve in the Second World War.
1950	The termination policy: the Federal government handed over control of Indian affairs to the states. Between 1954 and 1960 support to 61 tribes was cut off.
1969–71	The seizure of Alcatraz: the Indians tried to draw attention to their plight by direct action.
1973	The siege of Wounded Knee: a group of Indians seize the tiny hamlet and hold it against the police and state militia as a gesture of defiance.

Chiefs and Generals

COCHISE: Born 1812. Chief of the Chiricahua Apache in Southeast New Mexico. Terrorized the Southwest in the 1860s and 1870s. Made peace with General Howard in 1872 and remained true to his promise until he died in 1876.

CRAZY HORSE: Born 1840. Chief of the Oglala Sioux. Became a great leader after the Sand Creek Massacre (1864). Led the Indians at the Fetterman Massacre and Wagon Box Fight. Took part in the battle of the Little Bighorn. Surrendered at Fort Robinson in May 1877. Shot shortly afterwards while trying to escape.

CUSTER, GEORGE ARMSTRONG: Born 1839. Served with distinction in the Union Army in the Civil War. Became Lieutenant Colonel of the Seventh Cavalry in July 1866. Defeated the Cheyenne in the battle of the Washita in 1868. Took his regiment to Dakota territory in 1873. Killed at the battle of the Little Bighorn in 1876.

GERONIMO: Chief of the Chiricahua Apache. Born 1829. Second in command to Cochise. Became a great war leader in the 1880s. Captured by General George Crook in 1883. Greatest campaign in 1885–86. Surrendered in 1886. Imprisoned in Fort Pickens (1886–88), Mount Vernon Barracks, Alabama (1888–94) and Fort Sill, Oklahoma (1894–1909). Dictated his autobiography. Died in 1909.

HOWARD, OLIVER OTIS: Born 1830. Served with distinction in the Union Army during the Civil War. Made peace with the Chiricahua Apache in 1872. Lost nerve when faced by the rising of the Nez Percé. Died 1909.

CHIEF JOSEPH: Born 1840. Chief of the Nez Percé from 1873 to 1877. Refused to move his tribe to the Lapwai reservation until 1876. Tried to escape to Canada with his tribe. Stopped when within thirty miles of the border. Imprisoned in Fort Leavenworth, Kansas, and on Colville reservation, Washington, until he died in 1904.

MILES, NELSON APPLETON: Born 1839. Fought for the Union in the Civil War. Defeated the Cheyenne, Kiowa and Comanche in the Staked Plains campaign (1874–75). Defeated Sioux in 1876 and drove Sitting Bull across the border into Canada. Captured Chief Joseph and his band of Nez Percé in 1877. Forced Geronimo to surrender in 1886. Became Commander-in-Chief of the United States Army in 1895. Died in 1925.

RED CLOUD: Born 1822. Chief of the Oglala Sioux until 1881. Opposed the opening of the Bozeman Trail in 1866. Attacked Fort Phil Kearny in 1866 and 1867. Won treaty in 1868. Pushed into the background by Crazy Horse and Sitting Bull. Removed as chief because of his warlike activities. Died on the Pine Ridge reservation in 1909.

SITTING BULL: Born 1834. Chief and medicine man of the Hunkpapa Sioux. Became more and more important in the 1870s because of his visions. One of the leaders at the battle of Little Bighorn. Led his people into Canada rather than submit. Forced to return and surrender in 1881. Imprisoned in Fort Randall until 1883. Joined Buffalo Bill Cody's Wild West Show in 1885. Became involved in the Ghost Dance Movement in 1889. Killed while resisting arrest on the Standing Rock reservation, South Dakota in December, 1890.

Further Reading

THE best short introductions to the history of the North American Indians are J. Collier's *Indians of the Americas* (New American Library, 1947), and W. T. Hagan's *American Indians* (University of Chicago Press, 1961). A much fuller account is given in A. Debo's *A History of the Indians of the United States* (University of Oklahoma Press, 1970).

There are a number of very useful tribal histories. For the young, there is Sonia Bleeker's *Real Life Red Indian Series* (Dobson, London, and Morrow, New York), which contains books on the Apache, the Sioux, the Nez Percé and the Navaho among others. Among the best advanced studies are: G. B. Grinnell's *The Fighting Cheyennes* (University of Oklahoma Press, 1956); Francis Haines' *The Nez Percés* (University of Oklahoma Press, 1955); and G. E. Hyde's *Red Cloud's Folk: A History of the Oglala Sioux Indians* (University of Oklahoma Press, 1937).

There are two very good biographies of the great Indian leaders. Geronimo's own story is to be found in S. M. Barrett's *Geronimo's Story of his Life* (Duffield, 1906). Stanley Vestal has written a full account of Sitting Bull's adventures in *Sitting Bull, Champion of the Sioux* (University of Oklahoma Press, 1957).

Two of the main military figures have left their own accounts of what happened during the Great Indian Wars: General G. Crook, *Autobiography*, edited by M. F. Schmitt (University of Oklahoma Press, 1946) and General O. O. Howard, *My Life and Experiences Among Our Hostile Indians* (Hartford, 1907). Dee Brown has written an excellent account of the wars from the point of view of the Indians in *Bury My Heart At Wounded Knee* (Barrie & Jenkins, 1970 and Bantam, U.S.A., 1972).

Two illustrated histories of the American Indian are Oliver La Farge, *A Pictorial History of the American Indian* (Spring Books, London, 1956 and Crown Pubs., NY, 1956) and Matthew W. Stirling, *Indians of the Americas* (The National Geographic Society of America, 1955).

Notes on Sources

(1) G. P. Hammond and A. Rey, *Narratives of the Coronado Expedition*

(2) F. W. Hodge, *Spanish explorations in the Southern U.S.*

(3) G. Tucker, *Tecumseh: Vision of Glory* (Bobbs-Merrill, 1956)

(4) H. T. Malone, *Cherokees of the Old South* (Univ. of Georgia Press, 1956)

(5) F. Parkman, *The Oregon Trail* (Airmont, 1964)

(6) *Ibid*

(7) *Ibid*

(8) *Ibid*

(9) Chief Luther Standing Bear, *Land of the Spotted Eagle* (Houghton Mifflin, 1933)

(10) *Ibid*

(11) *Ibid*

(12) *Ibid*

(13) *Ibid*

(14) *Ibid*

(15) F. Parkman, *op. cit.*

(16) *Ibid*

(17) *Ibid*

(18) *Ibid*

(19) *Ibid*

(20) *Ibid*

(21) *Ibid*

(22) *Ibid*

(23) R. I. Dodge, *The Hunting Grounds of the Great West* (Chatto & Windus, 1877, and Putnam, 1877)

(24) R. B. Marcy, *Thirty Years of Army Life on the Border* (Harper Bros., N.Y., 1866)

(25) G. Catlin, *Illustrations of the Manners, Customs and Conditions of the North American Indians* (Chatto & Windus, 1876, Dover Pubs., 1972)

(26) R. I. Dodge, *op. cit.*

(27) Chief Luther Standing Bear, *op. cit.*

(28) *Ibid*

(29) *Ibid*

(30) *Ibid*

(31) F. Densmore, *Teton Sioux Music, Bulletin 61* (Bureau of American Ethnology, Washington, D.C., 1918)

(32) *Ibid*

(33) Chief Luther Standing Bear, *op. cit.*

(34) *Ibid*

(35) G. Catlin, *op. cit.*

(36) *Ibid*

(37) *Ibid*

(38) *Ibid*

(39) G. R. Stewart, *The Californian Trail* (n.p., 1844)

(40) U.S. Congress 39th, 2nd Session, *Senate Report 156*

(41) George Bent to George E. Hyde, 14th April, 1906 (Coe Collection, Yale Univ.)

(42) U.S. Congress 39th, 2nd Session, *Senate Report 156*

(43) *Ibid*

(44) *Ibid*

(45) George Bent, "Forty Years with the Cheyennes," *The Frontier*, Vol. IV, No. 6

(46) F. C. Carrington, *My Army Life and the Fort Kearny Massacre* (Lippincott, 1878)

(47) J. G. Neihardt, *Black Elk Speaks* (Univ. of Nebraska Press, 1961)

(48) R. Keim, *Sheridan's Troopers on the Borders* (McKay, 1885)

(49) E. S. Ellis, *The History of Our Country*, Vol. 6 (Indianapolis, 1900)

(50) Chief Standing Bear, *op. cit.*

(51) U.S. Congress, 44th, 1st Session, *House Executive Document 184*

(52) J. G. Neihardt, *op. cit.*

(53) T. B. Marquis, *Wooden Leg, A Warrior Who Fought Custer* (Univ. of Nebraska Press, 1957)

(54) *Ibid*

(55) General N. A. Miles, *Personal Recollections*

(56) S. Vendal, *Sitting Bull, Champion of the Sioux* (Univ. of Oklahoma Press, 1957)

(57) J. McLaughlin, *My Friend the Indian* (Houghton Mifflin, (1910)

(58) *Ibid*

(59) H. Garland, "General Custer's Last Fight as seen by Two Moon," *McClures Magazine*, Vol. II (1898).

(60) J. McLaughlin, *op. cit.*

(61) *Leavenworth Weekly*

Times, 18th August, 1881

(62) W. A. Graham, *The Custer Myth* (Stackpole, 1953)

(63) D. E. Conner, *Joseph Reddeford Walker and the Arizona Adventure* (Univ. of Oklahoma Press, 1956)

(64) *Ibid*

(65) *Ibid*

(66) U.S. Secretary of the Interior, *Report 1871*

(67) *Ibid*

(68) A. Debo, *A History of the Indians of the United States* (Univ. of Oklahoma Press, 1970)

(69) O. O. Howard, *My Life and Experiences Among Our Hostile Indians* (Hartford, 1907)

(70) S. M. Barrett, *Geronimo's Story of His Life* (Duffield, 1907)

(71) *Ibid*

(72) *Ibid*

(73) U.S. Secretary of War, *Report 1883*

(74) S. M. Barrett, *op. cit.*

(75) *Ibid*

(76) *Ibid*

(77) *Ibid*

(78) *Ibid*

(79) *Ibid*

(80) General George Crook, *His Autobiography,* ed. and annotated by M. F. Schmitt (Univ. of Oklahoma Press, 1946)

(81) S. M. Barrett, *op. cit.*

(82) *Ibid*

(83) Chief Joseph, *An Indian's Views of Indian Affairs* (North American Review, Vol. 128 (1879))

(84) *Ibid*

(85) *Ibid*

(86) L. V. McWhorter, *Yellow Wolf: His Own Story* (Caldwell, 1940)

(87) Chief Joseph, *op. cit.*

(88) *Ibid*

(89) *Ibid*

(90) *Ibid*

(91) M. Sprague, *Massacre, The Tragedy of White River* (Brown, 1957)

(92) *Ibid*

(93) U.S. Secretary of the Interior, *Report 1879*

(94) U.S. Congress, 46th, 2nd Session, *House Miscellaneous Doc. 38*

(95) *Ibid*

(96) U.S. Secretary of the Interior, *Report 1879*

(97) R. Emmitt, *The Last War Trail, The Utes and the Settlement of Colorado* (Univ. of Oklahoma Press, 1954)

(98) U.S. Secretary of the Interior, *Report 1877*

(99) *Ibid*

(100) K. E. Glaspell, "Incidents in the Life of a Pioneer," *North Dakota Historical Quarterly*, Vol. 8 (1941)

(101) J. McLaughlin, *op. cit.*

(102) *Ibid*

(103) *Ibid*

(104) *Ibid*

(105) *Ibid*

(106) *Ibid*

(107) J. H. McGregor, *The Wounded Knee Massacre from the Viewpoint of the Survivors* (Wirth Bros, 1940)

(108) *Ibid*

(109) Chief Joseph, *op. cit.*

(110) Chief Luther Standing Bear, *op. cit.*

(111) A. Debo, *op. cit.*

(112) *Ibid*

(113) P. Jacobs and S. Landau, *To Serve the Devil* (Vintage Books, 1971)

(114) American Indian Movement press statement, 8th November 1972

(115) Press statement by Carter Camp, co-ordinator of AIM, March 1973

(116) Stan Steiner, *The New Indians* (Harper & Row, 1968)

Index

Picture Credits

The author and publishers wish to thank the following for their kind permission to reproduce copyright illustrations on the pages mentioned: U.S. Signal Corps, frontispiece, 37, 75, 87, 98; Camera Press, 10–11, 46 *top* and *right*, 63, 68, 83 *top left*, 90, 106, 107, 108 *top* and *bottom*, 109, 110, 111; Smithsonian Institution, 12, 40 *top*, 51, 62, 76, 77, 97, 102 *bottom*; British Museum, 14, 16; The Weaver-Smith Collection, 18; Library of Congress, 20, 26, 49 *top*, 52, 57 *top* and *bottom*, 60–61, 66–67, 86, 91, 94, 100–101, 102 *top*, 103; C. M. Dixon Esq., 22, 45, 70, 83 *top left* and *bottom*; United States Information Service; 24, 32, 40 *bottom*, 59 *right*, 72–73, 74; Mary Evans Picture Library, 30, 39, 43, 49 *bottom*, 50 *left*; Nebraska State Historical Society, 34; Dennis Dobson Books, 42; National Museum of Canada, 46 *left*; Minnesota Historical Society, 50 *right*; Allied Artists Picture Corporation, 114; Victoria Picture Library, 115. Illustrations on pages 8, 15, 19, 21, 29, 31, 59 *left* and 84 are the property of the Wayland Picture Library.

The author and publishers also wish to thank Soona Hodivala, who drew the maps, and Times Newspapers Limited for permission to reproduce copyright material.

1 APR 1993

18 JUN 1996

Check
Spine
to Claim
+ correct.
DA

SURREY COUNTY LIBRARY

(Headquarters, 140 High Street, Esher)

SC-803055

This book must be returned to the Branch or
Travelling Library from which is was borrowed, by the
latest date entered above.

Charges will be payable on books kept overdue.